The Babushka Tree

Melissa Parenty

Ark House Press
arkhousepress.com

Cataloguing in Publication Data:
Title: The Babushka Tree
ISBN: 978-1-7642308-1-0 (pbk)
Subjects: REL012170   RELIGION / Christian Living / Personal Memoirs; REL012040   RELIGION / Christian Living / Inspirational; REL012150 RELIGION / Christian Living / Devotional Journal.

To connect with Melissa email: thebabushkatree@gmail.com
Facebook and Instagram: TheBabushkaTree

Design by initiateagency.com

This book is dedicated to the women and girls who are part of my very own 'Babushka' set: Alexandra, Sophie, Hosanna, Coco, Mia, Rachel, Angie, Lacey, Luna and Ahava - and those yet to join us who we cant wait to meet!

Contents

Introduction

My own experience as a great devourer of written words convinces me that chapter one must captivate the reader's imagination in such a way that they feel they simply must continue reading on to chapter two (even if someone has yelled at them in a grumpy manner to turn the light off, or told them that their eyeballs are hanging out of their head, or threatened them that tomorrow they will be no use for anything). This is opposed to closing the book after the first few pages and condemning the story to the place where all badly begun stories find themselves: tossed under beds next to rotting apple cores, pushed to the back of dusty, never visited bookshelves, or packed in boxes to be sent to charity.

Far be it from me to allow that to happen to this story, which I have waited many long years to write down. For this story has swirled around inside my mind for more than fifty trips of the earth circling the sun and it has reached a point that it simply refuses to stay inside my head any longer. I have been trying very hard to be good and do all the things that a responsible person should be busy doing, but it is no use. This story keeps crying out at me that it must get out of my head. So now I shall introduce you to a character who is very dear to me, and I am certain that once you have met him, you will be intrigued to follow this story into chapter two. And that once you have gotten that far along, commonly known in the book-loving world as the 'I couldn't put it down' point, you will find it necessary to keep reading on to find out how it all finishes in the end.

If, like me, you become so absorbed in a story to the point that you live and breathe momentarily in that imaginary world, falling in love with the characters, feeling their joy and sorrow like it is your own, then read on. My hope is that as you draw near to the final pages, you will slow down your reading speed, reluctant for the tale to end, because you will want to stay with my characters as long as you can – and finally when you turn the last page, your heart will be full of happiness and forever changed by the tale of the Babushka Tree.

Chapter One

Golden morning sunshine streams in through the window of the work shed where my elderly friend called by the name of Yousef sits, staring intently at the wooden object in his hands. His appearance is that of a grandfather: physical strength and grey-haired wisdom, with many smile wrinkles to betray his kind disposition. He exudes a joyful presence, for he is supremely happy being himself, doing exactly what he is meant to be doing, and doing it very well. His movements are filled with quiet confidence. Yousef is one of those people who can often be heard talking to himself and I find these types of people so much more interesting than silent people, for you can hear the things their brains are thinking, and it is like an invitation to get to know them better.

Presently, he speaks to the figure he holds in his hand: a bare wooden nesting doll that he had just finished sanding smooth. "Well little one, the time has come to give you your face." He pauses and his thumb strokes the doll's surface as he looks up at the shelf where several other gaily painted Babushka dolls sit in rows. They are waiting to be dispersed among the daughters of the families in the neighbouring township. Yousef works with his wife to create the Babushka dolls. He does the woodwork and as the doll takes shape, he conceives a vision for the face and decorative pattern. He describes it to his wife, who then brings his idea to life with a paintbrush.

Yousef speaks again to the doll in his hands. "I shall ask my wife to create for you a noble face, your dress will be made of sunflowers, and she shall paint a royal crown upon your head, for you shall be a queen who gives gifts to the broken hearted." He speaks as if he possesses a confident foreknowledge of the doll's destiny, and a determination that her image must be carefully painted to fulfil it.

Chapter Two

Several days later in early twilight we find Yousef placing a small wooden crate upon his work bench. Next to the crate lay a pile of clean calico cloths cut into squares and a bundle of pre-cut lengths of twine. One by one, Yousef takes down the nesting dolls from the shelf. Known around the world by their Russian names 'Babushka' (meaning grandmother) or 'Matryoshka'(meaning mother), these types of dolls are highly treasured for their craftmanship and beauty. With great care Yousef places them upon the bench. There are five sets in total; each set of Babushkas contains five dolls and has been named after the flower chosen for its unique design. The flower design is replicated over each of the varying sized dolls in the matching set.

As Yousef handles the doll named 'Rose', he smiles as he examines her closely. The doll has a pretty heart-shaped face with bright blue eyes, a pink rosebud mouth and golden hair. Her dress is red roses upon a yellow background. Carefully, Yousef pulls apart the set, down to the smallest, ensuring that their joins are smooth and fitting together nicely. As he rebuilds the Babushka set, he speaks out each doll's name. Beginning with the smallest he pronounces 'Baby Rose', who is enclosed by 'Daughter Rose', after that 'Mother Rose', then 'Grandmother Rose', and finally 'Matriarch Rose' who is the largest of the set and holds all the smaller dolls within her. His movements are careful, watching on we have the sense that he is handling objects of great value.

Yousef continues his final count of the dolls repeating the process of undoing, examining, and rebuilding, then just as he places the last doll back together the work shed door opens and through it enters Yousef's wife. A woman of small physical stature but large of heart and vigour, 'Mamie', as she is known to all, has come to light up the work shed with a lantern, and as you read further you will discover that in fact, she brings light wherever she appears. She is gentle, wise, and loving in both word and deed. She can say, "I love you," with a warm hug and show I love you with the practical work of her hands. It is her joy to work alongside Yousef and use her artistic skills to bring his visions to life.

Mamie's silver hair falls in gentle waves to her shoulders, and she wears a lilac woollen shawl to ward of the Autumn chill. With quick, gracious movements she mounts a step ladder, reaches up to hang the lantern upon the hook above the bench and speaks softly to her husband, "Yousef are you ready?" Turning towards her Yousef smiles at her and replies, "Yes Mamie the time has come. Our dolls are ready to leave their first home. Let us prepare them for their journey."

Mamie places herself in front of the square calico cloths and twine then looks expectantly towards Yousef who has the five sets of completed Babushkas lined up in front of him.

Until now my tale has been interesting but unremarkable, for we have simply discovered details and facts about our characters, but now I must ask you to open your heart to believe in wonderful things that some call fairy tales, others call wonderful mysteries and still others say that they are the very thing that life is all about.

Yousef takes a Babushka and places it upon his two hands which he holds as if he is holding an open book upon them. Looking down upon the doll he takes a very deep inward breath, then lifting the doll towards his mouth he exhales over the doll slowly. Yousef's eyes begin sparkling with a golden shimmer, and we see what appears like gold dust coming out of his mouth. As this gold dust falls upon the Babushka, it in turn glows for several seconds with the same sparkling light we see shining from Yousef's eyes. Once Yousef has finished his long breath, he passes the Babushka to Mamie who places a kiss on top of its head. As her lips touch the doll Mamie's silver hair glows brilliantly white and a type of dazzling electricity passes from her mouth onto the doll and illuminates the Babushka's face momentarily with a bright flash. After this Mamie reverently places the doll in the calico cloth and secures it with twine finished with a bow. She then places it upright in the crate and looks back to Yousef.

Yousef and Mamie repeat this process with the first four Babushka sets, until they have the final remaining Babushka doll set alone on the bench. This is the doll with the crown. She has emerald, green eyes, black hair and her design is bright yellow sunflowers upon a purple background. Mamie has succeeded beautifully in painting her a noble countenance, the dolls red lips smile as if she is bestowing a blessing upon you. "Our little Queen," says Yousef as he holds her in front of him. "You shall be the first chosen." She is breathed upon and kissed then wrapped and placed in the last remaining space in the crate.

Yousef and Mamie share a moment of contentment as arm in arm they look at their completed work. "Tomorrow we shall begin to find their new owners," Yousef announces with confident anticipation.

Chapter Three

Now we see our lovely couple seated closely for warmth on a wagon seat, in front of which a chestnut horse is clopping along at a swift walk. Puffs of steam can be seen escaping from the horse's nostrils as it breathes out in the crisp morning air. It is the magical time between the ending of the night and the birth of a new day. Stars can still be seen twinkling overhead, yet one senses that creation surrounding you is stretching its arms and yawning itself awake. It is best experienced outside, and if you are not sure what this feels like I encourage you to get up very early one day and try it soon.

The purity of chirping birdsongs combined with the fresh morning scents fill the hearts of our two sojourners with a reverent happiness. The road they are on cuts its way through farmlands as it winds its way down to the village called Damseldorf, which is beginning to stir into life as its inhabitants start their morning. Yousef glances at Mamie and begins to speak, "Today we shall be bringing our gifts to people with sad hearts. They have not long completed their harvest, and it has been a very disappointing one."

Indeed, the wheat farms of Damseldorf had been struck by unseasonal hailstorms one week before the fields were fully ripened. They were passing fields that looked as if a giant ogre had been trampling them underfoot. The harvest was pitiful and the villagers, most of whom relied upon the profits of one harvest to see them through to the next, were facing troubling times ahead. Normally harvest was a joyful time, at the end of which the annual village fete was held for several days and included much merry feasting and dancing. This year there would be no village fete, and it was only the very aged among them who could remember the last time this occurred.

As they travel closer to Damseldorf Yousef and Mamie begin seeing farmhouses closer to the road. They hear roosters crowing and the sound of bells as cows are being walked towards barns for morning milking. As strangers here, they are uncertain of the type of welcome they will receive. Presently Yousef calls out a greeting to a young boy they see walking near the road with empty milking buckets. He glances their way and stops walking. Yousef slows the horse to a stop. He smiles at the boy and speaks with a cheerful voice, "Good morning, we are strangers here looking to buy a good breakfast. Do you know of any farms who take in travellers?"

The boy answers swiftly, "Good morning. Yes, my mother is normally willing to offer breakfast to those who can afford to pay a silver coin." Yousef reaches inside his coat and withdraws a small coin pouch, which he jiggles as he replies, "Yes, we can do that. Is it possible for you to ask her if she is willing today?" The boy nods and quickly runs off in the direction of his house. Yousef and Mamie exchange a knowing smile.

Within minutes the boy is running back towards them with a determined look upon his face. "My mother is willing," he says with a happy voice then stands panting half bent over, for in his excitement he has exerted himself.

Yousef speaks again and says, "Well my boy, my name is Yousef and this is my wife, Mamie. And what might we be calling a strong lad such as yourself?"

"My name is Frances Smit," replies the boy. "I am thirteen years old and the eldest child of my parents. My father told me to lead you to our barn where I shall provide water and hay for your horse."

Yousef nods and replies, "How might you like to hop up here and drive us down to your barn?

Frances looks very surprised, then excited, and answers "That would be most wonderful, but I beg your pardon for I am still learning how to drive a wagon."

Mamie laughs as she responds, "Not to worry dear boy, our horse practically drives herself she is so clever. Jump up and Yousef will show you what to do." Frances climbs nimbly up to the seat where Yousef and Mamie have parted to make a space for him.

Yousef spoke kindly, "Now Frances, the thing about horses is they like you to talk to them, so when you take the reins I want you to introduce yourself to our girl Sugar and tell her where you are taking her."

Frances took the leather reigns from Yousef with a grin and spoke to the horse. "Hello Sugar, my name is Frances, but most people call me Frannie. I am going to take you to our nice warm barn, give you a brush and some water to drink, then some good oats. How does that sound?" Sugar's ears twitched and she snorted as if in reply. The three on the seat all laugh together in unison. Yousef suggests to Frannie that a light tap of the reigns with a, "Get on girl," will get them moving, and so it does.

Chapter Four

Yousef and Mamie soon found themselves seated at a well-worn wooden table in a cosy little kitchen. A busy mother named Greta speaks to them over her shoulder from her spot in front of the stove where she is cooking. "I'll be fixing you some griddle cakes I hope that will be to your liking?" She wears a calico apron over a simple grey dress made of flannel. Her hair is chestnut brown and pulled into one long plait, which hangs down to her waist and swings around as it follows her quick steps. Greta moves about her kitchen with vital energy, and her actions are efficient as every one of them is counting against the clock which she glances at as she works. Mamie replies, "That sounds lovely my dear. We hope that we are not adding too much of a burden to your morning, but we are very thankful to have something hot in our stomachs to start the day."

Greta allows a small smile as she replies, "Oh no trouble Mam, no trouble at all. I just beg your pardon if I cannot stay with you too long with the children underfoot and my husband who will be expecting me to help with the milking shortly." At that moment a tousled haired boy of ten years of age known as Lucas enters the kitchen closely followed by his equally tousle haired six-year-old brother George. They glance inquisitively at the guests as they walk to the other end of the table and seat themselves. The children appear clean and healthy, and they have a polite calmness about them which is an indication of their parents good training. Greta places plates on the table, with a bowl of jam and a larger bowl of cream. Frannie enters the kitchen, removes his boots and seats himself down next to his brothers. The three children look on hungrily as their mother places upon the table a large plate piled high with steaming griddle cakes. Yousef comments, "Now that is what I call home cooking!" he smiles at Greta, who looks very pleased.

As they begin their breakfast, Greta speaks, "Do you mind me asking what brings you to Damseldorf? I am hoping you are aware that our annual village festival has been cancelled due to the failed harvest?" She is presuming Yousef and Mamie are merchants who have come to sell their wares at the fete.

"Ah yes, we had heard of the terrible storms you have suffered. No, we are not here to sell goods. We are here to deliver some gifts." Yousef's answer causes Greta and the children to exchange glances of curiosity. For a little while everyone is busy with the happy business of eating. The hot griddle cakes are simple fare but delicious with a spreading of jam and a dollop of cream on top. The jam and cream are luxury items only used for special occasions, so the children are grateful that the guests have caused them to partake of an extraordinary breakfast. Through the kitchen window the sun begins to lighten the early morning sky.

After a little while Greta asks her guests. "So, do you know people here in the village?"

"Actually no, we do not," replies Yousef, and continues, "You see, we are artisans from a small village that borders yours, and together we make wooden Babushka dolls. When we heard about your village having a failed harvest, we decided we would bring some gifts to brighten the hearts of some of the young maidens who live here."

Mamie adds, "But it seems we have come to a house where you have been blessed so far with only sons to fill your table?"

"There is one daughter in this house," says Frannie. His mother looks at him with her face showing some veiled emotion. She arises from the table and begins to busily clear the plates.

"I have a twin sister. Her name is Flora. I was born first, and Flora took a long time to be born. She is blind, partly deaf, cannot use her legs and is unable to speak much," here Frannie stopped.

Greta stood with her back to the table. When she turned around her eyes were glistening, but she speaks with a brave smile. "Yes, we do have one daughter, she is our sweet girl named Flora. I must go to my husband now and help with the milking. Frannie, can you help Flora with her porridge and please give her one of the griddle cakes that are leftover. Yousef and Mamie I am sorry the breakfast was so simple, yet I hope it will give you the strength you need for the day ahead."

Yousef spoke, "No Greta, we thank you for your kind hospitality when you are so very busy." As he spoke, he rose from his chair and began to take his coin pouch from his jacket.

Lucas spoke, "Are you going to give out your gifts to the girls in the village today?" He had followed the conversation and was curious to know the visitors' plans.

Yousef answered, "Yes that is a work we plan to begin this day, but perhaps we may request to meet your sister before we leave, if your mother agrees?"

Greta who was busily pulling on her boots said, "It is as you wish, Frannie may introduce you. Please there is no need for coins for you are elderly and have come to help the village."

Mamie, who had risen from her chair and taken coins from Yousef's pouch stepped closer to Greta, reached for her hand and placed the coins in it. As she did so she said, "Dear Greta, we can see you are such a good little mother. We have set aside gifts to distribute, and it is our wish to share it with your family for you will have need of it in the months to come."

Greta looked down at her hand, her eyes widened with great surprise, and she replied, "Oh no, this is too much money for such a breakfast as I have served you." If the truth be told Greta had rarely held such an amount of money in her hand at once. The four silver coins were enough to feed her family for several months. Our lovely Greta is the type of strong woman who is so used to working hard to eke out a living that to be offered a generous gift felt rather overwhelming.

Yousef spoke, "Do not consider it payment for breakfast. Consider it a blessing from someone who knows what you need and can give it with joy." At this he stepped near to her and as if by magic pulled yet another silver coin out from behind her ear and held it out for her to take. The boys who were watching closely could not contain their polite silence and exclaimed with great surprise for Yousef was gifted at slight of hand tricks.

Greta burst into wonder filled laughter. Mamie spoke. "I know that good mothers have a place where they store provisions for difficult times. Put the coins there Greta and use them as you have need." Greta could see that resistance was not going to work with this determined couple. In her heart she knew that their future year ahead was going to be very challenging, and the idea of having those coins stored away would bring her untold relief from anxiety. In a flash of wisdom, she realised the only thing stopping her from accepting the gift was her pride at the idea of receiving help. Who knows, perhaps this couple had been sent to them for this very reason? She decided that she would accept the gift but had in mind to return it if they were able to survive without using it. After pondering a moment, she nodded and walked over to a kitchen cupboard, pulled down a pot and put the five coins in it. As if in a daze, she thanked Yousef and Mamie and held their hands as she passed them, then went out to help her husband.

Chapter Five

As his mother closed the door Frannie spoke to Yousef and Mamie. "Would you like to meet my sister?" He has known Yousef and Mamie for such a short period of time, yet he senses with youthful intuition that they are both exceptionally kind.

"We would like that very much," replies Mamie.

Frannie leads the way from the kitchen into a small dark hallway, they follow along as a little group, with the younger brothers behind.

The dwelling is not so large, there are three bedrooms. Frannie leads the way to the room that he shares with his twin. It holds two single beds and one closet for each of them, as well as a low wooden stool, which is used by the family when they attend to Flora. The walls are bare, apart from one simple wooden cross. There is one small window that looks out to the barn.

Within the bed on the right lay the slight form of a young girl. Upon her lower stomach lay a purring grey cat by the name of Whiskers who is being caressed by Flora's hands as she makes sounds that sound rather musical, a mix between humming and singing. She has a pretty face with delicate features, framed by chestnut brown curls that trail well past her shoulders. Upon hearing the sounds of footsteps entering her room Flora turns her head and smiles, and her blue eyes, though unseeing, sparkle with the light of life.

"This is Flora," says Frannie. They have all entered the small space and are gathered by her bedside.

Lucas pipes up and says, "Flora stays in her bed until she has had her breakfast, then mother helps dress her and she comes into the kitchen."

Little George also explains, "Flora loves the cat."

Mamie who is greatly affected by the sight of Flora bends down and places one of her hands lightly upon her cheek and speaks into her ear. "Hello Flora. My name is Mamie." At the touch of Mamie's hand Flora stops making her noises and turns her face towards them. Frannie is pleased to see his sister being treated with kind attention.

Because of her disabilities, and the fact that she cannot speak well, people often ignore Flora because they presume she is incapable of responding. In reality, Flora has a perfectly good brain and is very intelligent. Mamie continues to speak to her. "You are probably not used to having guests in your bedroom so early in the morning, forgive us, but we have a special reason for being here today."

Mamie speaks again, "Yousef perhaps you can fetch our crate from the wagon? I shall stay here. Frannie, I believe you were going to help Flora have her breakfast. If you agree I would be very happy to sit with you." Yousef leaves with Lucas and George who are feeling excited to follow him around. Whilst Frannie fetches Flora's porridge Mamie continues to speak with Flora. He returns with the breakfast on a special tray that his father had built. It has legs which allows it to sit like a tiny table over Flora's lap.

"Flora enjoys her breakfast best when I stay with her. That's why mother helps with the milking, and I stay here," explains Frannie.

With Frannie's expert help Flora sits up in bed and Whiskers the cat jumps down and saunters away. Frannie positions the pillows behind her back then places the tray table over Flora's lap and hands her the cloth serviette, which she places under her chin. She then explores the objects on the tray with her hands, a cup with water, her bowl of porridge, and upon discovering her extra plate with the griddle cake topped with jam and cream she smiles and claps her hands. Mamie and Frannie both laugh at seeing her delight. Needless to say, she chose to eat the griddle cake first, then moved on to her porridge.

Despite not being able to see, Flora was a remarkably tidy and quick eater. Just as Flora was finishing they heard Yousef and the children approaching, and George entered first with eyes twinkling with excitement. He rushed over to Flora and grabbed her hand speaking excitedly into her ear. "Flora, you are getting a gift from Yousef and Mamie."

Flora smiled and began to clap her hands again and she speaks for the first time in front of her guests saying in a soft voice, "Me, me, me?"

"Yes Flora, for you," announces Yousef happily. Frannie rises from the stool and invites Yousef to come sit in his place. Yousef seats himself with the crate of wrapped dolls on his lap. He bends near and speaks to Flora, "Flora, inside my crate there are five wrapped packages, and I would like you to choose one as your gift." He lifts the crate to the edge of the bed. Frannie takes Flora's hands and places them on top of the wrapped dolls. Flora explores the wrapped packages picking each one up and feeling them all over. Eventually, she settles on one and Frannie releases the twine bow so that Flora can unwrap her gift. As her hands feel their way to the wooden doll, her face is alight with excitement. The brothers look on with great interest to see what will emerge. Within the calico lay the Sunflower Babushka with the golden crown. Yousef and Mamie look at each other and smile.

The brothers exclaim at the craftmanship of the doll. "Oh, it is very fine, look at the crown."

Mamie describes the Babushka to Flora. "Flora, this is a Babushka doll. There are five dolls altogether that sit inside each other. Your set is called 'The Sunflower Queen', because she is painted with bright sunflowers all over and wears a golden crown on her head." As she listens to Mamie, Flora runs her hands all over the doll, then lifts it up, curiously feeling it from every angle. She runs her thumb along the line all the way around the doll where the two parts of the Babushka nesting doll are joined, then shakes the doll slightly. She has understood that something else lay inside. Youssef gently places his hands over Flora's and guides them to pull apart the largest 'Matriarch' Babushka. The next sized down 'Grandmother' Babushka doll slides out onto Flora's lap. The boys giggle at the look of great surprise that appears upon Flora's face. She feels for the two parts of the Matriarch Babushka, runs her hands all around them to explore the doll. She then lifts up the Grandmother Babushka, shakes it gently, smiles and pulls it apart so that the Mother Babushka falls onto her lap.

Flora's face is alight with discovery as she continues pulling apart the dolls until she comes to the final smallest doll that does not open. Upon realising that there is no opening Flora cups the smallest 'Baby' Babushka in her hands and gently rocks it from side to side, as if she is cradling a tiny baby, crooning softly. Yousef speaks. "You are right Flora. She is the smallest doll who must be looked after and protected." Mamie wipes a tear from her eyes as she watches on. Her brothers observe quietly as Flora begins to reassemble the Babushka set in perfect order, building up from the smallest.

"You are clever Flora," praises Frannie, speaking closely into his sister's ear so that she can hear him.

"Just wait until Father and Mother see this!" pipes in Lucas happily. Suddenly they hear a sound at the door and all turn to see Greta who is standing there with a beaming smile lighting up her entire countenance.

Chapter Six

So it was that Flora came to be the proud owner of the first of the five Babushka doll sets to be given out in Damseldorf by our friends Yousef and Mamie. It was no surprise to them that Flora had chosen the Sunflower Queen Babushka, and they were confident in the knowledge that soon wonderful things were going to take place in Flora's life.

After meeting Greta's husband Hamish briefly, leaving a slip of paper with their address and having bidden their farewells, we see Yousef and Mamie once more seated on top of their wagon, waving goodbye as they head off towards the village. Placed securely in the wagon we see the crate with the remaining four calico wrapped Babushka dolls. We shall not see our lovely couple until quite a bit later in this story, but when they reappear it will be perfect timing.

Meanwhile, we shall rejoin the Smit family, and I shall introduce you to the man of the house. It is nearing the lunch hour, and we find our good father Hamish still working in his barn.

It is from her father that Flora has received her curly hair. Hamish Smit has a head full of dark brown curls that are held down by his work hat worn for warmth in winter and to guard from the sun in hotter months. He wears a thick beard and when he takes off his hat he looks rather like a large grizzly bear, for he is tall in height and broad in stature. In the coming weeks he will be cleaning up his fields from the hailstorm damage and ploughing to prepare the ground for the next sowing of wheat. Right now, he is busy doing maintenance on his plough.

As he works, he has in mind the faces of Yousef and Mamie who he had met just before they left. He is wondering how these two people can have such big hearts for strangers they do not know. His wife Greta had told him earlier of this couple's great generosity in paying for their breakfast and adding a very large gift, as well as the handcrafted Babushka doll given to Flora. His heart has been very much encouraged by the visit from the travellers, and he pauses in his work to bow his head in a moment of grateful prayer.

Inside the house Flora has been dressed for the day and placed in her day chair in the kitchen where she is happily shelling peas. Greta is determined to give her daughter skills that will allow her to participate well in life.

Their usual routine after breakfast was to help get the boys ready for school, packing their lunch boxes and seeing them off on their way. The three boys all attend Damseldorf school, which receives students aged between five and sixteen years of age. The school is divided into three classes, which are age based, the younger class being aged five to eight years, the middle class being nine to twelve and the older class aged thirteen to sixteen.

George is in his first year and full of excitement to be heading off with his big brothers. He has been learning his alphabet with enthusiasm and diligence. Lucas, on the other hand, tends to find attending school an onerous task, which he would rather avoid; this shows in his reports with comments alluding to him being 'easily distracted' and 'talking too much'. Despite his reluctance to be formally educated, Lucas has a very clever brain and achieves high results without much effort at all. Frannie has a natural inclination towards intellectual learning so enjoys school and applies himself to his learning. He also achieves good results, but has to put a dedicated effort into it, as opposed to Lucas who seemed to be able to absorb facts by simply sitting in the classroom while his mind is elsewhere. George was in first class, with Lucas in the middle year, and Frannie just beginning the final level known as third class.

As Greta watched Flora diligently shelling the peas her heart ached for her daughter. Flora's life was extremely limited by her physical conditions of blindness and inability to walk, and she was unable to attend school. So far, Greta and Hamish had been unable to find any medical help to improve her condition.

As Greta did her morning chores with Flora, she was feeling unusually tired, and her hastily eaten breakfast was threatening to not stay down in her stomach. She presumed that it was the excitement and busyness of having unexpected guests to cater for. As she pondered these things Flora said in her sing song style of speaking short sentences, "All done, all done." Greta walked over to Flora and took the bowl of fresh green peas and poured them into the pot of simmering water prepared for them. She then gave Flora the bread dough that had been sitting to rise next to the oven and was ready to be kneaded. It was one of Flora's favourite jobs and she began pounding her fists into the white dough with enthusiasm, puffs of flour rising as she did so.

As she began to chop onions for the soup she was preparing Greta suddenly felt her stomach heave and ran to vomit up her breakfast in a bucket outside the back door. After it was over she remembered that the only other times this had occurred was when she was expecting a baby. She placed her hands to her stomach, and she worried about the already difficult year ahead considering the failed harvest. She would have news to tell her husband this evening when they were alone.

Chapter Seven

That night, as Hamish lay next to his wife in bed, she told him her suspicions of expecting another child. He accepted it stoically, pulling her close saying, "Perhaps our Flora will have a little sister at last." She admitted her fears to him about having enough provisions and the fact that she would be less available to assist him with farm work. He assured her that God had always provided for them in the past and would continue to do so if they trusted in him. Hamish was soon breathing in such a way that she knew he had already fallen asleep. She concluded that if his simple faith allowed him to rest peacefully then she should do the same, and after some quiet prayers, with her heart and mind now calm Greta also fell into a much-needed sleep.

Several days later Greta was outside working in the vegetable garden harvesting some carrots and herbs that she intended to use for dinner. Flora was sitting nearby on a blanket playing with her Babushka dolls. Greta paused in her busy work to watch her daughter. She was a pretty picture with the afternoon sunshine behind her, sitting underneath an apple tree. Flora had pulled apart her dolls and was playing an imaginary game. Greta could hear Flora making little sounds as she moved the dolls about, imitating speech to each other. As she picked up the smallest doll Flora spoke a word amongst her babbling that sounded very much like 'baby.' This was a new word for Flora, who had a very limited vocabulary. Greta continued to watch and listen. Flora continued her own 'language' but again, very clearly amongst the sounds Greta heard the word 'baby'. Dropping the bunch of freshly harvested carrots she was holding to the ground and brushing the dirt from her hands Greta walked quickly over to where Flora sat and knelt next to her. She put her hand upon Flora's hand that still held the smallest Babushka and speaking into Flora's ear said, "That's right Flora, baby." Flora turned her head at her mother's touch and smiled. She held up the tiny doll and repeated the word 'baby'. Greta felt like her heart would burst with joy, as each new word was a great achievement for Flora. She knew that Frannie had been practising repeatedly the words for each different sized doll with Flora. "You are clever Flora learning to say this new word." Flora smiled and spoke again saying, "Come, come," and pulled her mother closer and letting her hands feel their way to her mother's stomach to rest there, she repeated the word, 'baby'. In amazement Greta nodded and drew Flora into her arms weeping quiet tears of happiness. "Yes Flora, baby. Mother has a baby growing in there, a little brother or sister for you." Greta's mind struggled to make sense of how Flora could have known she was pregnant. How had it happened? In the distance they heard the sounds of the boys coming up the road on their way home from school. Greta could not wait to tell them the wonderful news of Flora's new word and the new family member to be expected.

That night as the family sat down for their evening meal, they held hands to say grace. Hamish spoke with heartfelt emotion. "Father in heaven we thank you for the miracle of new life, that we will have a baby coming to join our family. We thank you for Flora learning to say a new word. May you bless her to continue to learn more words. We thank you for this meal, and that you always provide our needs. Amen." There was great joy at the table that evening. The timing was perfect, as after the sorrow of the failed harvest the family had fresh hope for the future ahead.

Chapter Eight

The next morning Lucas approached his mother and asked if he might please borrow the Babushka dolls to take to school as they had 'Show and Tell' that week. Show and Tell was an opportunity for students to speak in front of the whole class. Lucas knew that the dolls were very valuable, and he liked the idea of having something impressive to show the class. Greta replied, "It is possible as long as you take great care, and do not allow the Babushka out of your sight." She knew that Flora would miss her dolls but thought that one day to share them with her brother was not really asking too much.

So it was that Lucas wrapped the Babushka set carefully in its original calico cloth, packed it into his schoolbag and headed off to school with a happy expectation of his day ahead.

As the boys walked along Frannie said to Lucas, "You must be extra careful with the Babushka, the dolls are very precious to Flora."

Lucas replied, "I know Frannie, I am not stupid." Who likes to be told what to do by their sibling, even if what they are telling you to do is the right thing?

It was just after morning tea when Lucas's teacher Miss Schlatter invited him to come to the front of the class for his turn of Show and Tell. The children looked on curiously as Lucas placed the calico wrapped Babushka on the table and spoke in a confident voice. "A few weeks ago, travellers stopped at our farm to buy breakfast. They were old and kind. The man's name was Yousef and the wife's name was Mamie. They gave us a gift."

Lucas carefully unwrapped the Babushka and set it on the table. The children in the class were suitably impressed, and there were comments of how beautiful it was, and how clever the craftsman must be. Lucas pulled apart the dolls and as he did so he explained, "This is called a Babushka. Yousef and Mamie give each set a name. Ours is called the Sunflower Queen, because of the flower and the crown. There are five dolls, the largest is called Matriarch because she is the biggest and carries the others. Next there is Grandmother, then Mother, Daughter and finally Baby, which is the smallest."

Miss Schlatter spoke. "They are very fine Lucas, I remember my grandmother had a set of these dolls that I used to enjoy playing with when I was a child visiting her house. Perhaps if Lucas is willing, we can allow you to pass the dolls around, but children you must be very careful with all the pieces." At this moment a student named Mary Owens excitedly put up her hand as if she were bursting with something important to say.

Lucas said, "Yes Mary?" Mary spoke. "There are four other girls in our school who also received a Babushka from these people. Charlotte and Abigail Brown, the twins in First class, and Georgia and Amy Vanderbrot who are cousins in Third class. I heard them talking about it in the playground," she added, feeling very important that she was the one to bring this additional information to her class.

Miss Schlatter was thinking to herself, "That is interesting, these gifts appear to have been given to the families in the school who have heavy burdens to bear. The five-year-old twins Charlotte and Abby have a very troubled home life with their father Bobby Brown the town drunkard, their mother with seven children under the age of twelve to care for. Georgia and Amy (Amy being an orphaned niece who had been taken in by her extended family) are suffering the sad decline in health of Georgia's mother Betty, who is dying of cancer. How did the elderly couple know?"

Lucas spoke, "Oh that makes sense, because they told us they were going to give out the other dolls when they left our farm." Lucas agreed to passing out the five dolls to children who had their hands raised, excited to be first chosen. The children were accustomed to Show and Tell rules and knew after they had a turn to pass the doll to their neighbour. Miss Schlatter wrote the word 'Babushka' on the blackboard and explained to the children that it was a Russian word that means grandmother.

A boy named David who was a student in the class known for his mean character and habit of misbehaving sneered as he was passed one of the dolls and said, "This is a girl's toy," and tossed it carelessly onto another student.

Lucas frowned at David who pulled a rude face in reply, and Miss Schlatter spoke to interrupt the unpleasant moment. "Babushka dolls are in fact designed to be both ornaments and toys that people of any age can appreciate and enjoy."

After all the class had looked at the dolls Lucas put the Babushka set back together, wrapped it carefully in its calico cloth and went outside to place it safely in his school bag. The class then had maths lessons and were afterwards released for lunch playtime into the school yard.

Damseldorf school consisted of three classrooms, a small teachers office and separate boys' and girls' bathrooms. It was placed on the edge of the village in a grassy meadow. There were lots of trees upon which the children delighted to climb, as well as plenty of space for skipping and ball games. Lucas was sitting with his friends eating his sandwiches underneath their favourite tree, when David approached with two other boys and taunted him. "There is Lucas, the boy who loves to play with dolls." The three boys snickered, and David added in a taunting tone, "Maybe he will be putting bows in his hair soon."

Lucas suddenly stood up and walked towards David, until he was directly in front of him. Although David was twelve years old Lucas was tall for his age, so they stood at level height. They eyeballed each other for a few seconds then Lucas spoke with his hands balled into fists at his side. "Stop your silly talk or you will be sorry." David pushed Lucas in the chest with two hands and in the next moment the two boys were scuffling and throwing punches. Children quickly gathered around to watch and cheer on Lucas, as apart from David's two friends (who only stuck with him because they were weak willed boys) the children would all be glad to see David taught a lesson.

Suddenly Frannie appeared in the middle of the circle and being much larger was quickly able to separate the boys and hold them apart. "No fighting in the school yard," he said loudly. Lucas had come out on top with no visible damage, however David had a bloody nose which he was wiping on his sleeve.

"You need your brother to rescue you huh?" David spat out, trying to salvage some pride.

Frannie spoke sternly, "You look more like the one who needed rescuing, and anyway as a school prefect it's my job to stop fights, it doesn't matter who." Speaking to Lucas he said, "You should know better, now apologise, shake hands and finish it." The children who had gathered had stopped their calling out and were now waiting in silence to see what would happen.

Lucas who was still panting and hot under the collar said, "He started it." Frannie folded his arms and stared at his brother without speaking. His eyes carried the message that Lucas had better do what he said or else. They had been raised to always do the right thing, no matter the behaviour of someone else.

Lucas held out his hand and said quietly, "Sorry David."

David just stared at Lucas, refusing to shake hands. He then turned and pushing his way through the other children who were staring at him he said over his shoulder, "You'll be sorry you ever hit me."

Frannie spoke to the children. "Nothing more to see here," and they began to disperse, talking to one another about what had just happened and agreeing that they were glad Lucas had managed to land a good hit. Frannie spoke again to Lucas once they were alone. "Steer clear of that boy, his father has a lot of power in Damseldorf and we do not want to create trouble for our family." It was true enough, David's father, Baron Bernard Cousteau was the wealthiest man in the village and owned a majority share of the buildings, businesses, and farms with many villagers subservient to him. A stern man who was driven by financial gain Baron Cousteau was a widower who had little time for his only child David. The local people agreed that The Baron had changed after he lost his wife to a horse-riding accident when David was a little boy of three years of age. The truth of the matter is that David is a heart broken, angry boy who does not know how to be kind, because he has been shown very little kindness since his mother died. He has known mostly sadness and loneliness, and because of his father's lack of interest has been left to be mostly raised by already overworked and poorly paid servants. I tell you these things because soon we shall see David behaving in a way that will reveal the dark places in his heart.

Chapter Nine

We shall follow David as he wipes his bloody nose on toilet paper in the boy's bathroom, planning revenge in his mind. He walks outside and checking that no one is looking, quickly runs to the row of school bags outside his classroom. Crouching low so as not to be seen, he makes his way to Lucas's bag, pulls out the calico wrapped Babushka and quickly unwraps it.

With lightning speed, he pulls apart the dolls down to the smallest, which he slips into his pocket. He then puts the doll back together, rewraps it in the calico and puts it back in the bag exactly as he found it. Checking every direction is clear, he exits the classroom and walks around the corner of the building which is closest to the teacher's office. He knocks on the door and Miss Schlatter calls out, "Come in." David opens the door to see his teacher sitting at her desk doing paperwork and holding a sandwich that she is eating at the same time. "Yes David?" she questions, noticing that he looks a little pale and spying remnants of blood on his cheek.

David said, "Lucas hit me, and I had a bleeding nose. I want to go home."

Miss Schlatter looks surprised, "Why did he hit you, David?" she questions.

David shrugs his shoulders and lies. "I don't know, he just ran up to me and hit me. Maybe he was angry that I didn't want to play with his dolls."

Miss Schlatter looks disconcerted, as she considers this possibility. It is true Lucas is not the perfect student, but he is not known for being a bully like David is. Her teacher sense causes her to suspect that David is not telling the whole story, and she decides she shall seek out the facts herself from other sources. She writes a quick note explaining that David has been given permission to walk home due to his bleeding nose and feeling unwell. As she hands David the note she says, "You are excused to walk straight home and rest this afternoon."

David walks home to his house, the most impressive one in Damseldorf being a large manor with extensive gardens, stables, and adjoining farmland. The front of the manor is surrounded by high wrought iron fences. Keeping a low-profile David quietly pushes open the large double gate. He then walks directly down the side pathway into the back garden, which is a secluded space, with many large trees and hedges creating plenty of hiding spaces. David glances furtively this way and that to ensure none of the servants are nearby, then he continues down past the rear of the large stables and finally arrives at the furthest edge of the yard, which leads into the manor farm fields. He pauses to check again that the coast is clear, then continues into the paddock, the one that contains an old orchard grove of huge, gnarly apple trees that have been left to their own devices, not having been cared for or harvested in many years. It is David's hiding place. The old apple grove holds the remnants of his only memory of his mother. It seems to him that he had been with her in this place as a tiny boy and in his mind he sees a picture of her smiling face holding out an apple for him to take. The trees are wildly overgrown in appearance, affording the perfect hide out for when David wishes not to be found by the servants.

Studying the trees, he walks towards the one situated at the bottom right-hand corner of the field. The giant old tree appears nearly dead, with very few green branches. He kneels beneath it and begins to dig a small hole in the soil. The task is not an easy one as the ground is hard and rocky, but David persists until he has reached a depth of about five centimetres. He then reaches into his pocket, withdrawing the brightly painted baby Babushka doll and places it in the hole saying, "You will be in the dark forever and no one will ever see you again." He then covers it over replacing the soil he has just removed, patting it down and doing his best to make it look like nothing has happened there.

Arising and brushing off his hands and knees he creeps away to his secret place; a disused harvesting shed at the northern corner of the orchard. Once inside he walks to the bench where he takes up a whittling knife and a small stick and sitting cross legged in the dirt he begins to carve. David has a true artist's gift, but right now he uses it in an unfortunate manner to create ugly, demon like creatures with leery, angry faces that mirror the swirling tide of bitter unhappiness going on inside his heart. When he hears the school bell ring for end of day in the distance, he will wait the amount of time it normally takes him to walk home, then enter the house as if he has been at school the entire day.

Chapter Ten

At the Smit farm Frannie, Lucas and George enter the house, removing their boots and jackets, and head straight to the kitchen. Their normal routine is to greet their mother and sister and eat afternoon tea, before heading to do afternoon chores. Lucas removes the calico wrapped Babushka from his bag, knowing that Flora will be happy to have her dolls back as soon as possible.

The kitchen is warm with smells of freshly baked cookies and a simmering soup. The cookies are a simple favourite known as Jamdrops. A recipe that involves making sweet dough balls that are indented by your thumb and in the hole is placed a spoonful of jam. Flora is sitting at the kitchen table wearing her apron which shows evidence that she has been working with both flour and jam, for she has been involved in the making of afternoon tea. The boys greet both their mother and sister with a kiss on the cheek and wash their hands before seating themselves at the table. Lucas places the Babushka doll in Flora's hands saying, "Here you go Flora." And addressing his mother he adds, "The Sunflower Queen was very popular in my class today Mother, thank you for letting me take it for Show and Tell."

Flora, who has flour on her cheek and is looking very cute because of it, smiles sweetly and claps her hands at being reunited with the dolls. With nimble fingers she unwraps the Babushka from its cloth and dissembles it. When she comes to the second last doll Daughter Rose her face takes on a puzzled expression. She gives the doll a little shake then frowns and speaks the word, "Baby?" as a question. The boys are looking on as they eat their Jamdrops. They watch Flora open the doll which would normally reveal Baby Sunflower but alas as you and I both know she is empty! Lucas jumps up from his chair and quickly looks through the doll pieces and shakes the calico cloth hoping that somehow the doll will be found. By now everyone is looking concerned, and Frannie speaks, "Lucas did you check that all the dolls were there after Show and Tell had finished?"

Lucas, whose face has gone pale answers, "Yes Frannie, I know I did because I was being very careful. I am sure that all five dolls were there before I wrapped it back in the cloth." Greta comes to the table and checks for herself if the missing doll is there, she then instructs Lucas to bring his schoolbag to the table. Greta makes a thorough search of the bag, in vain. By now Flora has a few tears making pathways through the flour on her cheek, and George has come to her side to comfort her by patting her hand.

Greta remains calm despite her fear that the smallest Babushka doll may have been lost. With a mother's discernment she has already concluded from the expression of sincere concern on Lucas's face that he is innocent of wrongdoing. Lucas speaks, "Mother I *know* the whole set was there, I don't understand what could have happened."

Frannie speaks, "I think I might have an idea." They look to Frannie as he continues. "Today at school Lucas got into a fight with David Cousteau." Lucas gives Frannie an accusing glance that communicates his displeasure at his brother telling tales on him.

Lucas exclaims hotly, "David started it, he was looking for a fight."

Greta interjects holding up her hand to stop further escalation between her boys. "Fighting is forbidden at school so we must obey the rules. Lucas no matter what David Cousteau did to provoke you, you have broken the school rules." Lucas hangs his head in defeat at his mother's logic, even though he is very angry inside.

From experience, he has learnt it is better to be quiet and receive a rebuke, than to protest his case with his mother. Frannie speaks, "Mother, Lucas did apologise and shook hands afterwards, but David refused to do the same."

Greta considers this information before pronouncing judgement. "I am pleased to hear that Lucas did that, however I must dissuade you from fighting again so you shall write me twenty lines of, "I will not fight at school," straight after your chores are done. Also, we must consider how to find the missing doll, Frannie do you think that David might be involved?"

"I am not certain, but it would make sense," Frannie answers. "He was mighty angry after the fight because Lucas got him good." At this phrase Lucas lifted his head and could not resist returning the smile that his brother was giving him, the sting of being told on was removed. Greta came to Flora and took both of her hands and put them palms facing together into the prayer position, communicating that this was a problem they would give to God for him to solve.

Chapter Eleven

Greta and Hamish discussed the situation and decided that they would ask Frannie to approach David at school and ask directly if he knew anything about the missing Babushka doll. They also prayed as a family together that God would help the Baby Sunflower Queen to be found and reunited with the other dolls.

After dinner while Lucas was writing out his lines, Frannie tried to explain to Flora what had happened. Flora kept shaking her head saying, "No," as her way of communicating her displeasure. She kept repeating, "Look baby, look baby," which Frannie knew meant that she wanted to search for the baby Babushka. Although Flora could not walk as her spindly legs held no muscle, she could drag herself around on the ground with her forearms, which she liked to do when she played on the floor. That evening, Flora used her hands in place of her eyes to explore every inch of the house. Dragging herself along the floor she pulled open every drawer she could reach, and investigated every nook and cranny, all in vain.

Frannie went to stop her, but Hamish said, "Leave her be son, she is determined, and I think she will be more peaceful later if we let her do this now."

As Frannie and Flora went to bed that night Frannie could hear Flora crying softly in her bed. Creeping over to her he knelt down, held her hand and spoke into her ear.

"Flora, I am going to find your doll. God will help me, please don't cry. Trust God, he will make a way." Flora placed her arms around her brother's neck and giving a deep shuddering sigh she finally relaxed, and her tears subsided.

In the meantime, something strange and supernatural was taking place over in the Cousteau's old apple orchard.

The near dormant, huge apple tree that had the baby Babushka doll buried at its base suddenly began to glow with a warm golden light. It is hard to explain and really you would have to see it yourself to truly understand how amazing the sight was, but I will try. The seemingly dead branches began to glow as if golden electricity was surging into them, fresh green leaves and then small apple blossom flowers began to appear, until the tree was throbbing with golden, living light and looked like it was covered in fresh snow so thick was the covering of blossoms. At the same time an amazing fragrance filled the air, sweet and perfumed.

In the Cousteau manor David had also fallen into a fitful sleep (for no person who stores up bitterness in their heart ever truly sleeps well). As he slept, tossing, and turning in bed, a golden glow shone in the distance through his bedroom window.

Chapter Twelve

The next day, Frannie was determined to confront David as soon as possible. He arrived at school early and then planted himself near the front gate of the school yard scanning the street. Time wore on and there was no sign of David. His two friends arrived, and Frannie asked them where David was, they simply shrugged their shoulders and said that he normally arrived just before the bell.

Frannie was beginning to think he would have to give up when he saw David in the distance, dawdling along kicking a rock as he approached. After a little while David looked up and spied Frannie, even from a distance Frannie could see David's body stiffen and freeze momentarily. He then appeared to pull himself together. As David entered the school gate Frannie spoke, "David I need to ask you a question. One of the Babushka dolls is missing from our set since Lucas showed it to your class yesterday. I want to know if you know anything about it?"

David had a hard expression on his face as he answered, "Why are you asking me? I barely touched the stupid things."

He kept walking past but Frannie grabbed his shoulder and spoke again, "The Babushka doll is our sister Flora's favourite possession. Last night she cried herself to sleep. I know you are mad at Lucas, but I ask you to think about Flora."

Frannie's tone was urgent, and it was obvious he was upset. David felt a triumphant flush of power, then wicked gladness inside his hard heart at hearing about Flora's sadness. Let someone else know what it is like to suffer. He didn't care one bit! He had only ever seen Flora from time to time from a distance, he did not know much about her because she had never been to school. He thought about Lucas punching his nose and his anger swelled afresh inside him.

He spat out to Frannie, "Don't touch me! I had nothing to do with it, now leave me alone or I will tell my father that you are bullying me."

Frannie released him, and an expression of concern crossed his face. "There is no need to do that. I am simply asking because we are trying to find it. If you say you were not involved, then I will ask my questions to the other students." David realised he had bluffed Frannie with his usual fear tactic of, "I'll tell my father." He often used this to get himself out of sticky situations, as all the children in the school knew that Baron Cousteau was the man of power in the village.

Turning away, Frannie added, "If you are lying to me right now, and later on change your mind you can return it to me secretly and no one will need to know it was you, you have my word." For a moment the boys' eyes locked, David then looked away, put his head down and walked to his class without looking back.

Chapter Thirteen

In the beginning David's heart was cold like a stone, and he barely thought about the baby doll buried in the old apple orchard. And when he did, he thought, "It serves them right," as people who commit cowardly actions must place the blame on someone else's shoulders. Life went on, the children at school stopped talking about it (although poor Flora's heart grieved) and other things became the talk of the playground. Like the hardship the failed harvest was causing. Some of the local farmers were unable to stay on and were leaving to start again in new places. There were children who came to school with very little to eat, and David sometimes felt a pang of conscience pierce even his hard heart as he ate through his plentiful lunch during the break.

One day he was just about to bite into his piece of beef pie when he felt a small hand tapping on his leg. He looked down in surprise to see Charlotte and Abigail Brown staring at him, their pinched little faces showing clear signs of hunger.

"Please David, do you have something to share with us?" spoke Charlotte, her big eyes fixed upon his pie. Now David as you know had not always been a cruel and mean boy and being taken off guard found himself experiencing a strange desire to give something to eat to these two little girls. Alas the pie was his last food, and his mouth was already watering. He found his head and heart battling but quickly made up his mind when he saw Lucas appear in his side vision.

"Go away you pests and let me eat my lunch in peace," he said in an angry voice.

The two little girls turned away sadly, and David heard, as Abby confided to her sister, "See I told you it would be no use, David Cousteau is the richest AND the meanest boy in school."

Somehow the pie lost its flavour as David sat there eating it.

Suddenly, in his mind, he saw the vision of his mother holding out the apple to him, smiling, and his heart gave a queer lurch. He stood up and called out, "Girls, come back." Charlotte and Abby turned around in surprise, looked at each other then walked back towards David. "Look, I don't have any other food today but tomorrow come and see me here and I will give you something." The girls' eyes were as wide as saucers as they nodded in stunned silence. The bell rang and all the children returned to class. David had a strange feeling going on in his heart that he had not felt for a very long time; it was the beginning of happiness.

Chapter Fourteen

Back at the Smit farm Hamish had managed to clear the failed harvest and was busily ploughing his fields to sow for the next season. Greta was growing rounder in the middle, and Flora was learning more words. One day Greta commented to her husband, "It seems to me that ever since Flora was given her Babushka doll she has begun to speak more." And yes, it was true. Flora was now able to speak several words in a row and make simple sentences. One of her often repeated ones was, "I miss my baby," which referred to her missing baby Babushka that lay sleeping in the earth in David Cousteau's old apple orchard.

Winter was fast approaching and the Damseldorf folk were talking much about how they could get through the cold months with their meagre supplies. Some of the more industrious farmers had preserved foods from past seasons that would help supplement their winter rations, however the poorer folk were struggling. The main problem was the lack of flour for bread. The large store in town had ordered in supplies from the nearest city, but it was being sold at such a high price that many could not afford it.

Greta had begun experimenting making a type of bread using ground oats, as she was able to purchase these cheaply from a merchant who passed by their home weekly. She was surprised by how good the simple recipe she created tasted. She had a few neighbours asking her if she could supply them with loaves in exchange for some of their preserved foods like tinned fruits and vegetables, smoked sausage and cheese.

Thus, Greta and Flora were kept busy every day grinding oats, baking the oatbread and exchanging with neighbours every few days. Greta found that the cost of the oats was much cheaper than what the exchanged items would be costing her at the store, so she was grateful to God that this idea had been birthed and was blessing her family with much needed supplies. So far, she had only used one of the coins from her special pot, so she was feeling hopeful that she may be able to return most of it back to Yousef and Mamie by next harvest.

Every night Frannie faithfully promised Flora that he would not give up the search for her doll, and they continued to ask their Father in Heaven to help them find her. Then one day, something happened that would see their prayers answered in a most wonderful way.

Chapter Fifteen

I t was the day that David Cousteau decided to sneak down to the old apple orchard before school to see if he could find a few apples for the Brown twins. Even though David's father was rich, he was not a generous man, and he checked his accounts with an eagle eye. This included the cook's expenditure, thus David was not allowed to help himself to the food supplies, but to eat only what was served or supplied. He had dared to allude to the hunger of some of the school children at dinner the previous evening and his father had slammed down his glass on the table and gone off in a tirade of how, "The poor are always asking for more." From this state of affairs David had rightly concluded that he would find no mercy from the cook by requesting extra food in his lunch pail. Thus, his plan to go foraging for apples had taken shape. David knew that the apple trees were not very healthy, as it was the wrong end of the season, and that finding a few edible apples would be a challenge.

As he walked past the stables in the frosty morning air he paused as he overheard the Groom speaking to the Gardener. "Mark my words he won't lift a finger for us poor folk." stated the Groom. "There he is living in all his finery, while our children are going to school with barely enough in their bellies to fuel them for the walk there and back!"

The Gardener, an older man with a deep voice replied, "The rich get richer, and the poor get poorer, so I was told, and my life bears witness to that fact. I have been paid the same wages for twenty years, never a penny more."

The Groom spoke again. "And it's not looking like it will change much with the next generation. My son tells me David Cousteau sits and eats his rich fare in front of all the other children without so much as offering them a crumb."

David felt his face flushing uncomfortably at this and walked slowly away to the apple orchard, pondering the words of his fathers' servants. His pride was stung and yet, the servants had never gone out of their way to show him much kindness either. It seemed like every man was for himself in this tough world, but as he thought that the face of Frannie Smit appeared in his mind saying, "I ask you to think about Flora." Frannie cared about his sister, and not just himself. David felt like he would rather not face this truth, because if he did, he might have to change his own mean ways. If he ignored the truth, he could just keep being the mean David Cousteau he currently was.

As he pondered these thoughts, he entered the old apple orchard and suddenly smelt the most beautiful and sweet fragrance in the air. Looking up in surprise he glanced around seeking to locate where it was coming from. The old, rather grotesque partly diseased apple trees could not be the source. Twisting this way and that David began following his nose and gave a loud gasp when breaking through some gnarled branches he beheld the sight of the now glorious apple tree where the baby Babushka doll was buried. He gave an involuntary cry out aloud as his mind struggled to understand. How could this be? The tree was now magnificently healthy and heavily laden with an abundant supply of large golden yellow apples. He was counting back the days in time, trying to work out how the tree could have gone from being bare one month previously when he had buried the doll, to now being laden with ripe fruit? David circled the tree warily, continually looking back towards the other bare trees right alongside then staring back at the Babushka tree.

Coming to a standstill in front of the tree, he walked forward in a now determined manner and kneeling at the base, began to pull back at the dirt, scraping his fingernails painfully against the rocky soil. He dug almost frantically, until suddenly his fingers felt the small, smooth surface of the baby Babushka doll. Pulling her out of the earth he examined the doll for damage as he brushed off the soil that clung to her sides. Wiping the doll completely clean on his shirt, he was surprised to see that her colours still shone gaily and that she did not appear to have suffered damage during her lonely month of exile in the ground.

David found himself speaking to the doll. "Who are you, what are you?" With care he placed the doll inside his top button up pocket in his jacket, then with his foot covered over the hole, return-ing the soil. Reaching up, David pulled an apple off the branch closest to him. He examined the skin - no traces of disease, no evi-dence of worm holes, in fact the apple looked perfect. Putting it to his nose he inhaled deeply. The fragrance of fresh, delicious apple was enticingly strong, and he found himself biting into it. The taste sensation exploded in his mouth. Bite after bite David gobbled up the apple in minutes and found himself staring at the core. "That was amazing," he said aloud, and before he knew it David had eaten three more.

Suddenly, feeling full and warm he slid down and leant against the tree. Gazing up into the branches above David's eyelids grew heavy and he slid into a half-awake dream. In the dream he saw his mother's form very clearly, she wore a white gown, and her skin seemed to glow softly with a golden hue. "David my son," she spoke kindly and gently. In the dream he felt her come very near, place her fingers beneath his chin and they looked into one another's eyes. "How I have missed you, how very deeply I love you."

As she spoke these words something that felt like a tightly held dam burst within him and David wept great tears of healing grief. In the dream he said, "Mother I have missed you too, and I long to be held by you." He sensed instantly that he was being held within her embrace, and David felt a great sense of safety and peace that he had missed for a very long time.

Then after what seemed just a moment his mother was again speaking to him, "David, you must return the doll to the broken-hearted girl."

"Yes, Mother I will," he promised earnestly.

Then she said, "And take this fruit to bless the unfortunate ones who are suffering." Again, he agreed to do as she instructed. Her last words were, "Take heart, now you shall live again, as do I." Then David was blinking himself back to consciousness under the tree. Wiping away his tears he stood and found himself smiling and laughing joyfully as he set to work gathering apples.

Chapter Sixteen

That day, David Cousteau turned up to Damselfdorf school pushing a wheelbarrow laden with the freshly picked delicious golden apples. Children came running as he entered the playground and stood there staring, waiting. David spoke in a loud voice, "I hope that each of you will take an apple from our orchard. As long as the tree keeps bearing them, I will bring this barrow every day to help you all have something extra to eat at school while we wait for better times." The children let out a loud cheer, and truly it seemed like the parable of Jesus feeding the five thousand, for the children seemed to keep coming and David was able to pass out an apple to each one, with no one missing out. When it came to the twins Charlotte and Abby David gave them each an apple and added, "Make sure you still come to see me at lunchtime," with a friendly wink. The little girls nodded happily as they ran off hand in hand.

The bell rang and it was time for class. Miss Schlatter who had witnessed the apple distribution and the change of behaviour in David smiled broadly at him as he came into the classroom. She was forgiving when less than 10 minutes later David had fallen fast asleep on his desk, tired out from his early morning exertions.

Later in the day, when it was the lunch break David sat in his usual place. It was not long before he was approached by curious children who wanted to hear the story of the apples. Where did he get them from? It was not the normal time of year for apples to be ripe how did it happen? Did he buy them from another country? And so on. They asked many questions, but David had to put them off for now as he knew he needed to return the Babushka doll before he could tell the true story.

After sharing some of his lunch meal with the twins, who had arrived with expectant eyes, David knew he must find Frannie before the break was over.

David walked over to the area where Frannie normally sat but could not see him. He was told by another boy that the Smit boys were not at school today, as they had to work on their father's farm this week.

As is often the case in rural areas, sometimes children are needed to help with seasonal workloads, and they must catch up with schoolwork when they get back.

David knew that meant he would have to find a way out to the Smit farm after school to return the doll, and the thought of facing the whole Smit family and confessing his sin made him feel weak at the knees and sick to the stomach. He considered putting it off for another day, but instantly his mind was filled with the vision of his mother's face, and he could again hear her voice saying, "You must return the doll to the broken-hearted girl." He decided with newfound conviction that he would have to go today before he might lose courage.

Chapter Seventeen

After the afternoon bell, David resolutely headed out the school gate in the direction of the Smit farm. He had never been there, only driven past in his father's automobile. Baron Bernard Cousteau was the only man in the entire region who owned one of the new contraptions that would eventually be replacing horse and buggies all around the country. Occasionally he took David for a drive on a Sunday afternoon, during which they spoke very little, as David had surmised that his father found his questions irritating and bothersome.

David was walking part of the way alongside Georgia and Amy Vanderbrot, who lived quite near the Smit farm. There was also Hans and Peter Grissel who lived just a short way down the road. Peter spoke to David as he turned off towards his house. "Those apples were so good; we hope you bring some more tomorrow like you promised. Bye David." David smiled. It was nice to be included. Most of his school years had been lonely and David had pushed other children away by his bullying and mean attitude.

Georgia also spoke to him. "Yes, David, it was very nice for you to do such a kind thing for everyone." She smiled sweetly in his direction as they walked along. Georgia was thirteen and appeared rather grown up to David as she was tall and wore her hair pulled up in a bun.

David had heard that her mother was very unwell. In a flash he realised that Georgia might be facing what he had already lived through, the loss of her mother. He glanced at her, and she noticed the sympathy shining in his eyes as he said, "If you would like to take an extra apple tomorrow for your mother you will be most welcome."

Georgia nodded and Amy spoke for them both when she replied, "That would be wonderful, yes we will be most happy to do that, see you tomorrow." They parted ways and David continued alone.

The closer he came to the Smit farm the more his legs felt like lead. He pondered how he would go about his visit. Perhaps he could ask to speak to Frannie alone? Yes, that would be the best way. Just do it outside, hand over the doll and get out of there as quickly as he could. Away from the shame of his awful act. When he imagined Mr and Mrs Smit learning about what he had done his cheeks burned red and he nearly turned around, but again he saw his mother's face flash into his mind, and he kept going.

Finally, he could put it off no longer, here he was at the Smit driveway. He walked towards the house, repeating under his breath, "Just do it, just do it," as he walked. He kept feeling the Babushka doll in his pocket, reassuring himself that it was there ready to be handed over.

He approached the door and knocked, his heart nearly beating out of his chest. Immediately he heard swift footsteps approaching and Greta Smit opened the door and David found himself being smiled at kindly. "Well, hello, David Cousteau! What a surprise, come in," she gestured and stepped back making way for him to enter in.

"Hello Mrs Smit," David spoke but did not move. "I am wondering if I might speak with Frannie?"

Greta answered, "Well yes that is possible, but probably not for a little while yet as they are finishing the milking. Do come in and wait."

David gave a reluctant sigh, as he realised there was no getting out of it now. With his head down David stepped inside. "Let me take your coat for you David," said Greta. "I have the fire going and you can come sit near it with Flora. At the name of Flora being spoken David again felt a flame of shame burning in his chest. David stared at Flora, who had turned his way. He remembered there was something not quite right with her but was unsure what it was.

Greta sensed his hesitance and tried to make him comfortable. "I do not think you have met Flora yet. Speaking into Flora's ear Greta explained, "Flora this is David who goes to school with our boys."

David stared at Flora as she spoke. "Hello David," and he realised that she was blind.

He replied, "Hello Flora, it is nice to meet you," as he drew near to sit on the chair offered by Greta. As he sat down, he noticed that Flora held the Babushka doll set in her arms, and his heart quivered inside his chest.

Greta spoke again. "Flora's Babushka doll is only out of her hands when she has chores to do, otherwise it is her constant friend and amusement." There was a small silence as David pulled his thoughts together. Greta sensed that the boy had something to say and watched him closely. Flora too was silent, as having a boy guest was a rare afternoon event.

David took a deep breath than began, speaking loudly so that Flora might hear. "Flora, I have come here today to return something to you." He unbuttoned his pocket and withdrew the baby Babushka doll. Standing up he approached Flora, opened her hand and placed the baby Babushka doll there gently.

Flora cried loudly, "My baby!" and tears of joy began to flow down her cheeks. David found his heart being squeezed very tightly as he watched on. With a rather shaky voice he spoke again, leaning closer. "Flora, I confess that I stole your doll. I was very angry at your brother Lucas, and I did it to spite him. It was very wrong of me, and I am sorry." He watched Flora, who despite her tears was smiling as she pulled apart the Babushka doll and placed the baby doll back inside.

Quickly putting the Babushka set back together she placed it on her lap. She then turned towards David and beckoned that he, "Come, come." David drew near to Flora, and she reached out unseeing for his hand. He understood and put his hand in hers.

She then took her other hand and patted his hand saying, "Good boy David. Brave boy David, God is happy. I am happy." At this very moment the back door opened and in came Frannie, Lucas, George and Hamish. There was a look of stunned surprise from them all to find David Cousteau standing there holding hands with Flora who announced, "David is a good boy."

Chapter Eighteen

To the credit of the Smit family, I must highlight how quickly they forgave David of his wrongdoing, for they were kind-hearted folk who knew that David had not had an easy childhood. How they marvelled and rejoiced at the story he shared about the miracle of the Babushka tree, and Flora glowed with happiness to think that it was because of her baby Babushka doll that the hungry school children were being fed throughout the lean winter.

That evening Frannie and Lucas sat next to David as Mr Smit drove David home in the wagon. Frannie spoke. "David if your father allows me I would like to come and help you gather the apples in the morning before school."

Lucas piped up, "Me too, but what about Flora's breakfast?"

Mr Smit who had overheard replied, "I think that George is getting big enough to be able to help his sister, you boys have my permission to do as you would like, for it will be of great benefit to

David to have your help. Just remember you will need to organise your time so that you are not arriving late at school."

So it was that at dawn the following morning the three boys made their way with the wheelbarrow towards what was now being called the Babushka tree. Both Frannie and Lucas were awed by the sight of the magnificent tree that appeared to be even more heavily laden with apples today than yesterday and Frannie exclaimed, "Truly this is a miracle!" They set busily to work, and once the wheelbarrow was full, they began pushing it back along the pathway. As they passed the stables the Groom caught sight of them and called out, "Hallo! What are you boys up to?" As he approached them his eyes grew wide with surprise when he saw the mound of delicious golden apples. "Well, what have we got here?"

David explained the Babushka tree story as quickly as he could, including the part that he had played, for the Smit's forgiveness had wrought its own miracle in David, and had given him courage to be honest and the Groom's eyes were full of wonder as he listened. "You don't say?" he kept repeating and shaking his head.

The boys excused themselves explaining that they were under strict orders from Mr Smit to not be late to school and left the Groom standing rather dumbfounded scratching his head as he watched them hastily rolling away their precious cargo.

You can imagine that it was not long before the entire village had heard the story. For the Groom told the Gardener, who told the Cook, who told the Fishmonger, who told the Pastor's wife when he delivered her fish and so on it went until it was the talk of the town.

That morning, true to his word, David gave Georgia and Amy the extra apple to be delivered to Georgia's mother and shared his lunch with the twins. David Cousteau was a new boy with a new heart.

The Babushka tree remained miraculously bearing fruit all through the cold winter months, supplying the children of Damselfdorf delicious golden apples daily until the next harvest.

And who could tell all the wonderful stories that grew out of this? There was the transformation of the Baron who upon hearing the story and walking down to see the Babushka tree for himself fell to his knees and wept healing tears also, for the apple orchard had been his pretty wife's favourite place and his stony heart was unlocked of its burden of grief and anger. He was henceforth a transformed man, who, rather than holding the townsfolk in a grip of oppression, became the benefactor who distributed the village bounty fairly and generously. He and David went to work together side by side with the servants to bring the apple orchard back to life.

There was the amazing story of the restoration of health to Georgia's sick mother, who after a steady daily diet of 'an apple a day' from the Babushka tree became well and left what was previously thought to be her deathbed to become vigorous and healthy once again.

And the twins' father, previously the town drunkard, who after eating just one of the apples from the Babushka tree given to him by Charlotte and Abby, resolved to become a better husband and father. He was promptly employed by the Baron to work in the Apple Orchard and became a trustworthy and reliable man.

Then we have David himself, who went on to turn his whittling into a noble art form that instead of ugly pieces, created wonderful imitations of local woodland creatures that were very popular with the village children.

Now, I did say that we would meet with Yousef and Mamie once again at an opportune moment, and that time is now. We see them rolling into the village of Damselfdorf one year since their last visit. This time, instead of storm devastated fields, we find fields of golden wheat shimmering in the sunshine ready for harvest. In the back of their wagon this year is a large object covered by a sheet. Yousef and Mamie turn into the Smit farm and as they approach the barn are greeted enthusiastically by the whole family, including new baby Grace who is held in her mother's arms with Flora being carried on her father's back 'piggyback style' as she refused to be left behind inside.

The family are bursting with the news of the miracle of the Babushka tree and Yousef and Mamie smile knowingly at each other as they listen with rapt attention. Greta speaks, interrupting her children who are vying with one another to tell all their stories, including Flora who has now turned into a nonstop chatterbox. "But you must be weary from your long drive, excuse us, come inside, we have prepared breakfast for you."

Yousef replies, "Before we do, we have come this year with another gift for Flora and if you agree we would like to give it to her now." The family watch as Yousef climbs up on the back of the wagon and uncovers the object. It is what looks like a chair on wheels, and the family look on with amazement as Yourself rolls it down some planks in front of them. He announces, "This is what is known as a wheelchair. Mamie and I saw one in the city when we were there and decided we would like to make one for Flora." The chair was made of wood that had been painted by Mamie with a bright, cheerful yellow. On the corners of the chair are two handles placed to be able to push it along. Yousef explains to Hamish how he had the idea of asking the blacksmith to make smaller wagon wheels to fit the chair. The boys' eyes are alight with excitement as Hamish carefully places Flora down to sit in the wheelchair. The honour of giving the first ride is given to Frannie. He moves forward very slowly at first, with Flora grinning with delight at the sensation of moving.

Frannie gains confidence and saying to Flora, "Hold on tight," he starts to jog along with Lucas and George running alongside and Flora begins laughing and giggling.

After everyone has had turns at giving Flora a ride, they move inside to have breakfast. After the festive and noisy meal, which of course had to include Greta's famous griddle cakes, Greta asks to speak with Mamie and Yousef alone. She began to say, "I want you both to know how much I appreciated your gift of coins last year. It truly was so kind, and it actually helped me in a surprising way." She paused as she pulled from her apron pocket a small bag containing ten silver coins. She continued saying, "With your coins, I was able to purchase oats and used it to bake bread throughout the winter. We had no wheat flour, and the flour available for purchase was excessively expensive. With Flora's help it ended up turning into a profitable exercise, and I am so happy to say that we can now be the gift givers back to you. I want you to take these ten coins as our way of expressing our gratitude." She held out the bag towards them. Yousef and Greta exchanged a swift glance during which no words were needed. When a couple have been married a lifetime, they have a knack of knowing what each other is thinking.

Yousef cleared his throat before replying, "Greta, what a noble lady you are, and we are delighted to hear that our gift helped make this possible. However, taking coins back from you we cannot do. A true gift is given in the spirit of not expecting anything in return. The joy we feel hearing of your good news is our reward."

At this Greta looked perplexed and Mamie added, "Greta how about you take these coins and use them to further your enterprise? The Good Book says, 'To those who have, more shall be given.' You have proven yourself to be a capable and trustworthy steward this past year, keep going and we shall be excited to come again next harvest and hear all about what happens."

Greta gave them both a hug and began to talk excitedly about the dream that had grown inside her this past year of opening a small bakery that could sell her breads and biscuits. They rejoined the rest of the family and the children talked excitedly about how wonderful it was going to be to take Flora to the Village Fete tomorrow in her new wheelchair.

I could keep telling stories forever about the Smit family, Yousef and Mamie, David and all the other children mentioned in this tale, however, here is where I, Flora, must say goodbye. Before I do, I have saved my favourite part of this tale for the very end. I too experienced a miracle after eating quite a few of those apples that David shared out. My blindness was cured and so it was that I was able to write this story down for you. I apologise that it has taken me such a long time to do it, but I am sure you will understand that after growing up to become a schoolteacher, marrying David Cousteau then raising our five children I have not had a lot of spare time to sit and write it all down.

The
Babushka
Tree

BIBLICAL REFLECTION JOURNAL

Chapter One

Text and character focus: Yousef

> 'He exudes a joyful presence, for he is someone who is supremely happy being himself, doing exactly what he is meant to be doing and doing it very well.'

To reflect upon:

> This text describes Yousef as a person who is happy because he is truly himself, doing what he is uniquely gifted to do, and delighting in doing it well.
>
> 1/ Ask yourself, "Have I ever experienced moments like this? Where was I? What was I doing?"

_____

_____

_____

_____

2/ If I am yet to experience this. Get excited! God has uniquely gifted you with creativity to bless this world and those around you.

_____

_____

_____

_____

_____

Scripture to meditate upon:

"Each of you should use whatever gift you have received to serve others, as faithful stewards of God's grace in its various forms."
1 Peter 4:10 -11 NIV

Prayer:

Dear Heavenly Father, thank you for the unique creativity, gifts and talents You have placed within me to share on this earth for Your glory. Please open my eyes to discover what they are and provide me the opportunities to use them. In Jesus' Name, Amen

Chapter Two

Text and character focus: Babushka dolls

> 'As he rebuilds the Babushka set, he speaks out each doll's name. Beginning with the smallest he pronounces "Baby Rose", who is enclosed by "Daughter Rose", after that "Mother Rose", then "Grandmother Rose" and finally "Matriarch Rose" who is the largest of the set and holds all the smaller dolls within her.'

To reflect upon:

> This text speaks of matrilineal lineage.... the amazing reality of God's design. Grandmothers, mothers and granddaughters are physically linked. This is proven scientifically.... when a female fetus is aged just 20 weeks' gestation she already carries the next generation within her tiny body.

1/ If you are female ask yourself, "Whose womb was I in as an egg inside my mother's fetus?" If a mother already, "Who did I hold within my womb, as a baby inside my mother?" If male, ask yourself, "What can I learn about my heritage from this amazing information of matrilineal lineage?"

_____

_____

_____

_____

_____

Scripture to meditate upon:

"For You created my inmost being, you knit me together in my mother's womb. I praise You because I am fearfully and wonderfully made, your works are wonderful, I know that full well." Psalm 139: 13-14 NIV

Prayer:

Dear Heavenly Father, I am in awe of your complex design in female matrilineal lineage. Thank You for opening my mind to this reality. Help me comprehend that You are the Creator of all life. Bless me to be able to understand Who You are, and who I am as one of your children. In Jesus' Name, Amen.

Chapter Three

Text focus: Just before dawn

'It is the magical time between the ending of the night and the birth of a new day. Stars can still be seen twinkling overhead, yet one senses that creation surrounding you is stretching its arms and yawning itself awake. It is best experienced outside, and if you are not sure what this feels like I encourage you to get up very early one day and try it soon.'

To reflect upon:

Sometimes we may go to bed at night with very tired, even anxious or sad thoughts, but find when we wake in the morning these have been washed away with sleep, and we find ourselves refreshed and happy to start a new day. The start of a new day brings fresh hope, like a fresh new page or blank canvas that has nothing written on it yet.

1/ Ask yourself, "How do I feel about the idea of a brand-new day, a fresh page or a blank canvas? Ponder....do I feel excited to live and create new things, or am I more worried and fearful about the future?"

_____

_____

_____

_____

_____

2/ Dream.... what is something I would like to have happen in my future that would be wonderful and even miraculous?

_____

_____

_____

_____

_____

Scripture to meditate upon:

"Let the morning bring me word of Your unfailing love, for I have put my trust in you. Show me the way I should go, for to you I entrust my life."
Psalm 143: 8 NIV

Prayer:

Dear Heavenly Father, thank you that You are the Creator of all that is seen and unseen, in heaven and on earth. Thank you for the gift of my life, and creativity to explore your world and learn and grow every day. Help me wake every morning with fresh hope in my heart and live a joyful and creative life. In Jesus' Name, Amen.

Chapter Four

Text and character focus: Greta

'Her hair is chestnut brown and pulled into one long plait that hangs down to her waist and swings around as it follows her quick steps. Greta moves about her kitchen with vital energy, and her actions are efficient as every one of them is counting against the clock, which she glances at as she works.'

To reflect upon:

These sentences describe Greta as a person who is working quickly, energetically and efficiently. She is also keeping a close eye on the clock. Greta is managing many tasks at the same time. She is cooking breakfast, being hospitable, feeding her family and extra guests, organising her children and getting ready to do farm work with her husband as her next task.

1/To ponder…. because Greta was a well organised, hard-working person she was able to receive unexpected guests. Ultimately, she and her family were greatly blessed because of her willingness to open her home to others, showing hospitality. Greta was also good at time management and managing her resources. Reflect upon this and consider if there are things about the character of Greta worth imitating.

_____

_____

_____

_____

_____

Scripture to meditate upon:

"Whatever you do, work at it with all your heart, as working for the Lord, not for human masters, since you know that you will receive an inheritance form the Lord as a reward." Colossians 3:23

Prayer:

Dear Heavenly Father, thank you for the gift of work, to be fruitful and productive. Help me learn to enjoy working hard and faithfully. Bless me to be ready to receive the special opportunities you send to me to serve others, even when I am busy with my own tasks. In Jesus' Name, Amen.

Chapter Five

'Frannie fetches Flora's porridge while Mamie continues to speak with Flora. He returns with the breakfast on a special tray that his father had built. It has legs which allow it to sit like a tiny table over Flora's lap. "Flora enjoys her breakfast best when I stay with her. That's why mother helps with the milking, and I stay here," explains Frannie. With Frannie's expert help Flora sits up in bed and Whiskers the cat jumps down and saunters away. Frannie positions the pillows behind her back then places the tray table over Flora's lap and hands her the cloth serviette, which she places under her chin.'

To reflect upon:

This section of text describes the way Frannie serves his twin sister Flora. He has a daily task of helping Flora have her breakfast. This involves him preparing her breakfast tray, bringing it into her room, assisting her to be comfortable and well positioned to eat, as well as providing her company by staying with her as she eats.

Frannie is showing some great character qualities by being willing to serve his sister, to treat her with kindness and respect, and sharing his presence with her so she is not alone. It is obvious that Frannie loves his sister. He is also taking up his responsibility as part of a busy family, doing his part to allow the family morning routine run smoothly.

1/ To ponder…. it is important to think about the special people God has placed in our lives and consider how we can serve them. As human beings we live in communities and have an active part to play in them. Groups, teams, and families work best when each person is an active participant who willingly contributes. There is a well-known saying, 'Be a fountain, not a drain'. What does this mean to you?

_____

_____

_____

_____

_____

Scripture to meditate upon:

"Be devoted to one another in love. Honour one another above yourselves."
Romans 12:10 NIV

Prayer:

Dear Heavenly Father, thank you for the people you have placed around me in my life, and the different communities that I am part of. Help me to develop a servant heart like yours, to love people well in the way I speak to them and my actions. Help me understand the ways I can play an active part in contributing. In Jesus' Name, Amen.

Chapter Six

Text and character focus: Hamish

'As he works, he has in mind the faces of Yousef and Mamie who he had met just before they left. He is wondering how these two people can have such big hearts for strangers they do not know. His wife Greta had told him earlier of this couple's great generosity in paying for their breakfast and adding a very large gift, as well as the handcrafted Babushka doll given to Flora. His heart has been very much encouraged by the visit from the travellers, and he pauses in his work to bow his head in a moment of grateful prayer.'

To reflect upon:

This section of the text speaks about Hamish and his personal reflections after meeting Yousef and Mamie. Hamish has been greatly impacted by the generous strangers, and he is feeling encouraged. After considering these things, Hamish takes a pause in his busy work to say a prayer of thankfulness.

1/ To ponder.... Hamish is a person who takes time to think, to reflect, and to pray. Sometimes in our technology focused lives, we can fail to leave time to do this. Quiet time, without noise, without others, being still and allowing our thoughts to meander and consider what has been going on. Think about when you find this easier to do, where are you and what are you doing?

_____

_____

_____

_____

_____

2/ After his time of reflection, Hamish turns to prayer. He realises that God is ultimately the source of every blessing in his life, and his heart is flowing with thankfulness. Remember when you feel blessed to take time to thank God.

_____

_____

_____

_____

_____

Scripture to meditate upon:

> "Every good and perfect gift is from above, coming down
> from the Father of the heavenly lights, who does not change
> like shifting shadows."
> James1:17 NIV

Prayer:

> Dear Heavenly Father, thank you that you are behind every
> blessing that comes to me. Please help me be a person who
> takes time to be still, and to reflect upon who you are and
> all the ways you are working everything together for good
> in my life. I want to be someone who remembers to thank
> you. In Jesus' Name, Amen.

Chapter Seven

Text and character focus: Family

'That night as the family sat down for their evening meal, they held hands to say grace. Hamish spoke with heartfelt emotion. "Father in heaven we thank you for the miracle of new life, that we will have a baby coming to join our family. We thank you for Flora learning to say a new word. May you bless her to continue to learn more words. We thank you for this meal, and that you always provide our needs. Amen." There was great joy at the table that evening. The timing was perfect, as after the sorrow of the failed harvest the family had fresh hope for the future ahead.'

To reflect upon:

In this section of text, we see the family being blessed by the announcement of a new family member on the way, bringing fresh hope for the future. This is especially encouraging after the stress and disappointment of the failed harvest. There is a saying that 'God works in mysterious ways,' implying that it can be challenging for we human beings to understand his plans when we are in the middle of something extremely difficult yet also touchingly beautiful at the same time.

To ponder:

1/ Have you ever been through an experience that was difficult, then arrived at the other side of it and realised you had learnt a lot, somehow been blessed through the process (despite the very real and legitimate trials) and developed some pretty epic character traits all at the same time? With God there is always an element of mystery that we cannot fully grasp, and this is a good thing. It proves that he is God, and we are not.

_____

_____

_____

_____

_____

_____

Scriptures to meditate upon:

"When I applied my mind to know wisdom and to observe the labour that is done on earth – people getting no sleep day or night – then I saw all that God has done. No one can comprehend what goes on under the sun. Despite all their efforts to search it out, no one can discover its meaning. Even if the wise claim they know, they cannot really comprehend it."
Ecclesiastes 8:16- 17 NIV

"For my thoughts are not your thoughts, neither are your ways my ways," declares the Lord. "As the heavens are higher than the earth, so are my ways higher than your ways, and my thoughts than your thoughts."
Isaiah 55:8-9 NIV

Prayer:

Dear Heavenly Father, thank you that you are God and that your ways are the best – even when I am struggling to believe through a difficult trial. Help me to trust you. Increase my faith and grow my assurance that you are always in control and working all things together for good. In Jesus' Name, Amen.

Chapter Eight

Text and character focus: Lucas

'Suddenly Frannie appeared in the middle of the circle and being much larger was quickly able to separate the boys and hold them apart. "No fighting in the school yard," he said loudly. Lucas had come out on top with no visible damage, however David had a bloody nose which he was wiping on his sleeve. "You need your brother to rescue you huh?" spat out David, trying to salvage some pride. Frannie spoke sternly, "You look more like the one who needed rescuing, and anyway as a school prefect it's my job to stop fights doesn't matter who." Speaking to Lucas he said, "You should know better, now apologise, shake hands and finish it." The children who had gathered had stopped their calling out and were now waiting in silence to see what would happen. Lucas was still panting and hot under the collar said, "He started it." Frannie folded his arms and stared at his brother without speaking. His eyes carried the message that Lucas had better do what he said or else. They had been raised to always do the right thing, no matter the behaviour of someone else. Lucas held out his hand and said quietly, "Sorry David."

To reflect upon:

Here we encounter a scene, which helps us understand the power of good parental training as well as the positive influence of an older sibling. Lucas is in the midst of a very difficult trial, and his character is being tested. David has ridiculed and taunted Lucas, and Lucas responds out of his natural instincts, to defend himself. When his older brother Frannie intervenes, Lucas is reminded of how he has been raised to 'always do the right thing' and given the opportunity to reconsider his actions. Admittedly, Frannie puts the pressure on, but sometimes we need that – a person to prompt us towards righteousness.

To ponder:

1/ Have you had moments when you have been tempted, but remembered the training of your parents, or the advice of someone you trust, and it has steered you towards making good choices? Or have you had someone in your life who has reminded you of 'doing the right thing'? Who was it, a sibling, a friend? Where were you, and what was going on?

_____

_____

_____

_____

2/ People of Christian faith who have put their trust in Jesus Christ, have the wonderful advantage of being trained by God's own Holy Spirit. This training occurs inside of us, within our hearts and minds. Sometimes we can be thinking about a course of action, and we experience a type of 'check' in our spirit, like a spiritual prompting. Sometimes a verse of Scripture will come to our thoughts, or we hear God's voice speaking within us. It is vitally important to listen and allow ourselves to be guided towards righteousness, which simply means 'right' choices. Remember, God never condemns when he speaks to us or uses shame or ridicule. He speaks in ways that convict us and cause us to really want to make good choices.

_____

_____

_____

_____

_____

Scripture to meditate upon:

"My sheep listen to my voice, I know them, and they follow me. I give them eternal life, and they shall never perish, no one will snatch them out of my hand. My Father who has given them to me is greater than all, no one can snatch them out of my Father's hand. I and the Father are one."

John 10:27 – 30 NIV

Prayer:

Dear Heavenly Father, thank you that you speak to me and guide me in making right choices. Train me to hear your voice above all others. Speak Lord, for I am listening. In Jesus' Name, Amen.

Chapter Nine

Text and character focus: David

The giant old tree appears nearly dead, with very few green branches. He kneels beneath it and begins to dig a small hole in the soil. The task is not an easy one as the ground is hard and rocky, but David persists until he has reached a depth of about five centimetres. He then reaches into his pocket, withdrawing the brightly painted baby Babushka doll and places it in the hole saying, "You will be in the dark forever and no one will ever see you again." He then covers it over, replacing the soil he has just removed, patting it down and doing his best to make it look like nothing has happened there.

To reflect upon:

In this chapter we encounter David committing an act of revenge by stealing the baby Babushka doll. His intent is to cause harm and hurt others. The Bible teaches us that what is going on inside of us will eventually come out and be displayed by our actions. It is described as a tree bearing good or bad fruit. David is bitter, hurting and angry and his actions show it.

To ponder:

1/ Prior to an action there is always thought. David must have thought about what he was going to do, then put that idea into action. Often someone may claim, "I didn't mean it" or "It wasn't my fault," after making a bad choice, however this is not the truth. God has given humanity freedom to make their own choices.

_____

_____

_____

_____

_____

Scripture to meditate upon:

"When tempted. No one should say 'God is tempting me.' For God cannot be tempted by evil, nor does he tempt anyone; but each person is tempted when they are dragged

away by their own evil desire and enticed. Then, after desire has conceived, it gives birth to sin, and sin, when it is full-grown, gives birth to death."
James 1:13-15 NIV

Prayer:

Dear Heavenly Father, thank you that you have given me freedom to make my own choices. Teach me to know when my thoughts are heading off track, away from righteousness. Train me to reject evil. In Jesus' Name, Amen.

Chapter Ten

Text and character focus: Greta

> 'Greta came to Flora and took both of her hands placing them together into the prayer position, communicating that this was a problem they would lift up to God for help to solve.'

To reflect upon:

> In this selection of text, we witness the terrible discovery that the baby Babushka doll is missing. After questioning her sons to understand what has happened, Greta's response is to turn the problem over to God in prayer. God does not want us to fret, worry or be anxious. He does not want us to lose our peace. He loves it when we bring our problems quickly to him, so he can help us supernaturally. This means that God can release his power into our situation. It is like a secret weapon, an advantage, or in gaming terms a 'hack'. Why wouldn't we use it?!

To ponder:

1/ When you face problems to solve, are you in the habit of turning to God for help?

_____

_____

_____

_____

_____

2/ What do you think is the better option:

A) to try and fix things yourself, then when you can't to eventually pray for help.

B) As soon as you face a problem, bring it to God and ask for his help straight away.

_____

_____

_____

_____

_____

Scripture to meditate upon:

"Do not be anxious about anything, but in every situation, by prayer and petition, with thanksgiving, present your requests to God. And the peace of God, which transcends all understanding, will guard your hearts and your minds in Christ Jesus."
Philippians 4:6

Prayer:

Dear Heavenly Father, thank you that you are always ready and willing to hear my prayers and help me find solutions. Train me to turn quickly to you and seek your help when I face problems of any kind. In Jesus' Name, Amen.

Chapter Eleven

Text and character focus: The tree

> The near dormant, huge apple tree that had the baby Babushka doll buried at its base suddenly began to glow with a warm golden light. It is hard to explain and really you would have to see it yourself to truly understand how amazing the sight was, but I will try. The seemingly dead branches began to glow as if golden electricity was surging into them. Fresh green leaves and then small apple blossom flowers began to appear, until the tree was throbbing with golden, living light and looked like it was covered in fresh snow so thick was the covering of blossoms. At the same time an amazing fragrance filled the air, sweet and perfumed.

To reflect upon:

> Have you ever watched time lapsed film of something growing? This is when a normally very slow process

unobservable to the human eye is painstakingly filmed over a long period of time. Then when we watch the film, we see in minutes what normally takes thousands of hours to unfold. This section of the story describes the supernatural bursting into life of the apple tree. It is a glorious vision for the eyes and provides a sense of wonder, because naturally an apple tree takes months and months of growth to go through this process – but in this story it happens in just a few paragraphs!

To ponder:

In real life growth takes time. An apple tree grown from a seed can take up to ten years to bear fruit. Puts things into perspective doesn't it! If grown from a grafted seedling it will take three to five years, this is still quite a long time. Apple trees bear more fruit when they are cross-pollinated from other varieties of apple trees planted nearby.

1/ Think of yourself as a tree. God is the master Gardener who is tending you. He provides the sun, rain and nourishment for your growth. He protects you from pests and storms. He is patient and understands that good fruit takes time to grow.

_____

_____

_____

_____

_____

2/ Now think of yourself as an apple tree, planted in an orchard among other varieties of apple trees nearby. This is a picture of a Christian believer planted in a church. We need one another to grow and bear lots of fruit.

_____

_____

_____

_____

_____

Scriptures to meditate upon:

"Blessed is the one who does not walk in step with the wicked or stand in the way that sinners take or sit in the company of mockers, but who meditates on his law day and night. That person is like a tree planted by streams of water, which yields its fruit in season and whose leaf does not wither – whatever they do prospers."
Psalm 1:1-3 NIV

"The righteous will flourish like a palm tree, they will grow like a cedar of Lebanon; planted in the house of the

Lord, they will flourish in the courts of our God. They will still bear fruit in old age, they will stay fresh and green, proclaiming 'The Lord is upright; he is my Rock, and there is no wickedness in him.'"
Psalm 92: 12-15 NIV

Prayer:

Dear Heavenly Father, thank you that as my loving Creator you look after me, tend me, protect me, feed me and nurture me. Bless me to be well planted among good people to grow strong and bear much fruit. In Jesus' Name, Amen.

Chapter Twelve

Text and character focus: David

'He made out to keep walking past but Frannie grabbed his shoulder and spoke again. "The Babushka doll is our sister Flora's favourite possession. Last night she cried herself to sleep. I know you are mad at Lucas, but I ask you to think about Flora." Frannie's tone was urgent, and it was obvious he was upset. David felt a triumphant flush of power, then wicked gladness inside his hard heart at hearing about Flora's sadness. Let someone else know what it is like to suffer! He didn't care one bit! He had only ever seen Flora from time to time from a distance, he did not know much about her because she had never been to school. He thought about Lucas punching his nose and his anger swelled afresh inside him.'

To reflect upon:

There is a saying that 'hurt people hurt people'. David is hurting, not just from the schoolyard incident with Lucas, but from previous sad things that have occurred in his life, like the death of his mother and his father's lack of love. David doesn't know what to with his sadness, anger and pain, and somehow it causes him to want to make someone else suffer.

To ponder:

Hard, sad and bad things happen to everyone, because of sin. Sometimes it happens to us, and sometimes we are the cause. People can create big problems in their own lives, and it can spread to others, because they don't know what to do with their painful experiences in life. God knew that, and he wanted to provide a solution to all that suffering. He sent his only son Jesus, to save us from this suffering.

1/ Sometimes when people first hear the Gospel, and they learn that sin is real and that they are part of the problem, they think it is Bad News. They don't want to think of themselves as having done something wrong, but we all do things wrong sometimes. It would be Bad News if the story ended there, and there was no solution to the problem of sin in the world, but thankfully it doesn't. The Good News of the Gospel story is that Jesus was willing to take the problem of sin and all the suffering in the world upon himself on the cross. He has made a way for sin and suffering to be dealt with.

_____

_____

_____

_____

_____

Scripture to meditate upon:

"Surely he took up our pain and bore our suffering, yet we considered him punished by God, stricken by him and afflicted. But he was pierced for our transgressions, he was crushed for our iniquities; the punishment that brought us peace was on him, and by his wounds we are healed." Isaiah 53:4-5 NIV

Prayer:

Dear Heavenly Father, thank you for the Good News of the Gospel, that you sent your son Jesus to be the Saviour of the world. Thank you that we can bring our sin and suffering to the cross, where Jesus takes it from us and deals with it. Thank you that we can keep bringing our sin and suffering every time we need to. In Jesus' Name, Amen.

Chapter Thirteen

Text and character focus: the heart

'In the beginning David's heart was cold like a stone, and he barely thought about the baby doll buried in the old apple orchard. And when he did, he thought, "It serves them right," as people who commit cowardly actions must place the blame on someone else's shoulders.'

To reflect upon:

A person described as having a heavy, cold or stony heart is not diagnosed with an incurable condition. It can best be understood as a temporary situation - put in another way, as if their heart is momentarily frozen. When a person is in this state, their emotions and feelings are blocked, they are unable to feel them properly. God knows how to safely 'break open' the hard human heart, or to thaw it out, so that it can be soft and responsive again, restored to feel, interpret and process emotions in a healthy way.

To ponder:

Physically speaking our hearts keep us alive, pumping the blood through our veins. From the viewpoint of our feelings, our heart plays an equally vital role in staying emotionally healthy.

1/ Life on earth can be very tough. Think about a time when your own heart felt heavy, hard or frozen, usually it will be in connection to feelings of sadness, grief, loss, disappointment or anger. Now think about a time when your heart felt light, soft and responsive to love and joy. What caused you to feel that way?

_____

_____

_____

_____

_____

2/ It is possible for us to manage our heart health, both physically and emotionally. Just as we can choose to eat healthy foods, exercise, get enough sleep and manage stress so that our hearts can be physically strong, so too we can look after and manage the emotional state of our hearts. The first step is to realise that this is possible. Some theories on this subject tell people that they are at the mercy of their emotions, that they are unable to manage them. God's Word teaches us that with God we can.

_____

_____

_____

_____

_____

Scriptures to mediate upon:

"I will give you a new heart and put a new spirit in you, I will remove from you your heart of stone and give you a heart of flesh."
Ezekial 36:26 NIV

"Above all else, guard your heart, for everything you do flows from it."
Proverbs 4:23 NIV

Prayer:

Dear Heavenly Father, thank you for the gift of my heart, that it pumps the blood around my body keeping me alive, and it also enables me to be connected to you and feel emotions. Thank you that as a Christian I have the promise of being given a new heart that can be soft and responsive to your truths. Teach me wisdom, help me to manage my emotions in healthy, life-giving ways. In Jesus' Name, Amen.

Chapter Fourteen

Text and character focus: The baby babushka doll

'Flora was now able to speak several words in a row and make simple sentences. One of her often repeated ones was, "I miss my baby," which referred to her missing baby Babushka that lay sleeping in the earth in David Cousteau's old apple orchard.'

To reflect upon:

The baby babushka has been buried in a temporary grave and is described as 'sleeping' beneath the apple tree. When David was in the act of burying the doll he says, "You will be in the dark forever and no one will ever see you again.". God's enemy Satan attempted to do this to Jesus, when he died on the cross. Jesus really did die and was buried in a tomb with a huge stone being rolled in front of it, including Roman guards placed to guard it. However, we all know the

Good News! That Jesus was resurrected on the third day, conquering sin and death. Likewise, the baby babushka doll is resurrected from her sleep beneath the apple tree, and wonderful events occur because of it.

To ponder:

Sometimes we go through seasons of life in which we can feel like we are 'buried' or like we are 'on the shelf' or in sporting terms 'on the bench'/ 'on the sidelines'. We must be very careful to hold onto our faith in God during these challenging times, to trust that He has a good plan for our lives, and that resurrection is coming.

1/ Think about someone you know or have heard about, or perhaps even a time in your own life, involving a season of being sidelined/put out of action. Think about the sense of being 'asleep' or 'sidelined'. Now think about how things unfolded and moved forward. How did resurrection occur? What did it look like?

_____

_____

_____

_____

_____

2/ God loves it when we trust and believe in his promises.
Decide today that if you find yourself in a season of life
where you may feel temporarily 'buried', or sidelined, that
you will trust God to bring resurrection. He will do it.

_____

_____

_____

_____

_____

Scriptures to meditate upon:

"Jesus said to her, 'I am the resurrection and the life. The
one who believes in me will live, even though they die, and
whoever lives by believing in me will never die.' Do you
believe this?"
John 11:25-26 NIV

"For we believe that Jesus died and rose again, and so we
believe that God will bring with Jesus those who have fallen
asleep in him."
1 Thessalonians 4:14 NIV

Prayer:

Dear Heavenly Father, thank you for the Good News of the Gospel, that our sins can be forgiven through Jesus' death and resurrection. Thank you that when we place our hope in your Son we can trust for resurrection power in every part of our lives, both now and for eternity. In Jesus' Name, Amen.

Chapter Fifteen

Text and character focus: David's mother

'In the dream he saw his mother's form very clearly, she wore a white gown and her skin seemed to glow softly with a golden hue. "David my son," she spoke kindly and gently. In the dream he felt her come very near, place her fingers beneath his chin and they looked into one another's eyes. "How I have missed you, how very deeply I love you." As she spoke these words something that felt like a tightly held dam burst within him and David wept great tears of healing grief. In the dream he said, "Mother I have missed you too, and longed to be held by you." At this he sensed instantly that he was being held within her embrace, and David felt a great sense of safety and peace that he had missed for a very long time. Then, after what seemed just a moment, his mother was again speaking to him, "David, you must return the doll to the broken-hearted girl."

"Yes, Mother I will," he promised earnestly. Then she said, "And take this fruit to bless the unfortunate ones who are suffering." Again, he agreed to do as she instructed. Her last words were, "Take heart, now you shall live again, as do I." Then David was blinking himself back to consciousness under the tree.'

To reflect upon:

In this encounter David's mother brings the healing, truth and guidance to her son that he so desperately needs. Firstly, she assures him that he is deeply loved, then she instructs him on what he needs to do to make things right, lastly, she instills the hope of eternal life in her parting message.

To ponder:

People need to know they are loved and valued before they will listen to and obey someone's instructions. In parent to child relationships this plays out especially during the teenage years when emerging young adults are beginning to exercise independent decision making. If teens do not feel loved and valued, they probably will not listen to or obey the advice that comes to them from those in authority, whether that be parents, teachers or others. After David is reassured of being deeply loved, he is able to receive his mother's instructions to return the baby babushka doll and share the apples from the tree with his hungry peers at school.

1/ God assures us that we are deeply loved through the Gospel story. God does not say, "Once you are good enough, then I will have a friendship with you." No, while we are lost, wretched, hurting, confused and broken hearted (Like David) God reaches out to us, reassuring us with his love, to save us. Because we know we are deeply loved, we can listen to our Heavenly Father's instructions and obey.

_____

_____

_____

_____

_____

Scripture to meditate upon:

"But God demonstrated his own love for us in this: While we were still sinners, Christ died for us."
Romans 5:8 NIV

Prayer:

Dear Heavenly father, thank you that you loved us first. Thank you that the Gospel message reassures us how very deeply you love us. Help me to take in your love, so that I can trust and obey. In Jesus' Name, Amen.

Chapter Sixteen

Text and character focus: David

'David knew that meant he would have to find a way out to the Smit farm after school to return the doll, and the thought of facing the whole Smit family and confessing his sin made him feel weak at the knees and sick to the stomach. He considered putting it off for another day, but instantly his mind was filled with the vision of his mother's face, and he could again hear her voice saying, "You must return the doll to the broken-hearted girl." He decided with newfound conviction that he would have to go today before he might lose courage.'

To reflect upon:

Here we find David facing his moment of temptation to either put off what he knows he must do or go ahead and get it done. Thankfully David aligns with his 'newfound conviction' and decides to press on and follow the prompting of his heart before his courage fails him.

To ponder:

We all face decisions every single day that matter. We constantly face varying temptations to either do what we know deep down, in conviction, what we should do, or 'put it off', procrastinate, avoid, deny, and so on.

1/ Think about someone you know who is 'true' to their convictions. If they say they are going to jog three times per week, they do it. If they claim to be a Christian, they go to church regularly, read their bible and tithe their money faithfully. If they say they don't swear, they don't. If they take a sick day from work, they are really sick and don't fake it. What do you admire about this person?

_____

_____

_____

_____

_____

2/ Now think about someone who cannot hold to their convictions, who makes big promises but doesn't follow through, who claims to believe something, but their actions do not align, who talks big but fails to show the evidence in their life. Why is it hard to trust this person?

_____

_____

_____

_____

_____

Scripture to meditate upon:

"For the Spirit God gave us does not make us timid but gives us power, love and self-discipline."
2 Timothy 1:7 NIV

Prayer;

Thank you, God, that you want to help us live good lives and that you can help us be overcomers of temptation. Please help me to stay true to my convictions, to be motivated to do the right thing, and to walk in your power and love. In Jesus' Name, Amen.

Chapter Seventeen

Text and character focus: Flora

'David drew near to Flora, and she reached out unseeing for his hand. He understood and put his hand in hers. She then took her other hand and patted his hand saying, "Good boy David. Brave boy David, God is happy. I am happy." At this very moment the back door opened and in came Frannie, Lucas, George and Hamish. There was a look of stunned surprise from them all to find David Cousteau standing there holding hands with Flora who announced, "David is a good boy."

To ponder:

Here we will focus on Flora's response to David's confession of wrongdoing. Flora has been heartbroken about her missing baby babushka doll, and wept many tears over it. She has been the victim of David's unfair and cruel actions.

However, immediately after David confesses, we witness Flora being quick to forgive, and to praise David for his repentance.

1/ How are you with forgiving others? Are you quick to forgive or do you hold grudges?

_____

_____

_____

_____

_____

2/ Think about Flora's excellent example of forgiving David and not holding it against him. She even decides to praise David, instead of talking about his poor actions and rubbing it in. Her response allows David to receive forgiveness and to recover from his shame.

_____

_____

_____

_____

_____

Scriptures to mediate upon:

> "Bear with one another and forgive one another. If any of you has a grievance against someone, forgive as the Lord forgave you. And over all these virtues put on love, which binds them all together in perfect unity. Let the peace of Christ rule in your hearts, since as member of one body you were called to peace, and be thankful." Colossians 3:13-15 NIV

> "My dear brothers and sisters, take note of this. Everyone should be quick to listen, slow to speak, and slow to become angry, because human anger does not produce the righteousness that God desires."
> James 1: 19-20 NIV

Prayer:

> Dear Heavenly Father, thank you for forgiving us for our sins and failures. Help me to be someone who is quick to forgive and ready to love. In Jesus' Name, Amen.

Chapter Eighteen

Text and character focus: Yousef and Mamie

'When a couple have been married a lifetime, they have a knack of knowing what each other is thinking. Yousef cleared his throat before replying, "Greta, what a noble lady you are, and we are delighted to hear that our gift helped make this possible. However, taking coins back from you we cannot do. A true gift is given in the spirit of not expecting anything in return. The joy we feel hearing your Good News is our reward.'

To ponder:

In this story Yousef and Mamie are the gift givers. They gift the Babushka dolls, money and a wheelchair for Flora. They are highly intentional about being generous and together delight in giving things away to bless others. In this section of text we understand the joyful secret of their giving: having no ulterior motives. This allows them to give freely and happily, because they are not driven by selfish motives to get something in return.

1/ Who do Yousef and Mamie remind you of?

_____

_____

_____

_____

_____

2/ Consider how Yousef and Mamie prepared the dolls as gifts to give away. They spent much time and their own provisions in designing and crafting the dolls, as well as wrapping them and travelling to distribute them. Think about something you might be able to give away as a free gift to others less fortunate than you are. Be intentional and give freely.

_____

_____

_____

_____

_____

_____

Scriptures to meditate upon:

"Every good and perfect gift is from above, coming down from the Father of the heavenly lights, who does not change like shifting shadows." James 1:17 NIV

"Remember this: Whoever sows sparingly will also reap sparingly, and whoever sows generously will also reap generously. Each of you should give what you have decided in your heart to give, not reluctantly or under compulsion, for God loves a cheerful giver."
2 Corinthians 9:6-7 NIV

Prayer:

Dear Heavenly Father, thank you for all the good gifts you give to me. Help me to be a generous gift giver like you are. In Jesus' Name, Amen.

Dolls in dolls

www.dollsindolls.com.au / also on Facebook as Dolls in Dolls

I reached out to this company so that my readers can receive a FREE gift when ordering their very own Babushka dolls!

Use code coupon: TREEBOOK

Contact the author:

You can contact Melissa through socials: The Babushka Tree

Or email her directly: thebabushkatree@gmail.com